IN PRAISE
OF TEDDY BEARS

'From early times the bear has commanded a special place in folklore, myth, fairy-tale and legend. It has been regarded as representative of both divine and natural forces; and today, in the form of the Teddy Bear, it is grasped in psychic compensation and clung to for security. The reason for this is that the bear functions as a powerful symbol that provides satisfaction for a widespread psychological need. Consequently, history, religion, philosophy and psychology are all involved in any proper explanation of the mystique of the Teddy Bear.'

COLONEL BOB HENDERSON
Bear Tracks, Autumn, 1977.

'Of all the otherwise mundane objects which stir our collecting instinct, from cigarette-cards to bottle tops, nothing provokes so much sentiment as the sight of an old battered Teddy Bear. The subject is such an emotional one that it is easy to overlook the fact that commercially Teddy has been the world's most successful toy.'

CAROL ANN STANTON
Art & Antiques, March 1978.

IN PRAISE
OF TEDDY BEARS

PHILIPPA & PETER WARING

Designed by Christopher Scott

PICTORIAL
PRESENTATIONS
SOUVENIR PRESS

This book is for our children
RICHARD, SEAN & GEMMA
and
COLONEL BOB HENDERSON
—because they all love
Teddy Bears

CONTENTS

A Hug of Welcome   6
Introduction: The World of Arctophiles   9
The Teddy Bear's Ancestors   15
The Father of the Teddy Bear   19
Who Made the First Teddy Bear?   25
The Adventures of the Roosevelt Bears   33
An A–Z of Some Famous Bears   41
The Real Truth About Winnie the Pooh?   54
The Vain Teddy   57
Miss Waterlow in Bed   58

Comical Teddy Bears   59
The Animated Bear   71
Some Hugs of Teddy Bears   75
The Making of Teddy   88
The Teddies' Book of Records   91
The Teddy Bear Club   103
The Fantastic Appeal of the Teddy Bear   119
Teddy Bear Tales   126
Acknowledgements   128

A HUG OF WELCOME

Grrreetings to the reader from some well-known Teddy Bears around the world! Starting from the top left hand corner on page 6 and going around the pages in a clockwise direction these are the bears. First, a sidelong glance from Jack Cramer's 'Teddy' busy with his honey pot in Ohio. 'Archibald Ormsby-Gore' the intrepid bear belonging to Sir John Betjeman who has been immortalised in verse and wrote to the authors that he was 'delighted you are producing a book on his fellow bears'. A signed photograph of New Zealand's most famous bear, 'Littlejohn' busy at his piano practise in Mark Steele's home. The much-travelled 'Oliver Q. Dodger', who has been all over the world with the Batchelor family, shown here enjoying his hobby of ski-ing. An elder statesman among teddies is 'Bear' who has lived with Jock Roper for over 70 years and here poses with his owner's favourite pipe. Industrious greetings from 'Worker Teddy' one of Japan's army of hard-working bears. Studious 'T. Dan Bear' who has helped his owner, Alison Callum in her work as a Senior Probation Officer in Lancashire, and signed his photograph with a paw-mark. 'One-Eyed Connolly' who lives in a tough neighbourhood of New York but gives much comfort to Mrs Helen Walton. And, finally, 'Theodore', Peter Bull's famous teddy studies his horoscope and wrote to us 'I would be curmudgeonly of me not to wish you all success with your book!' So welcome from them all!

Littlejohn

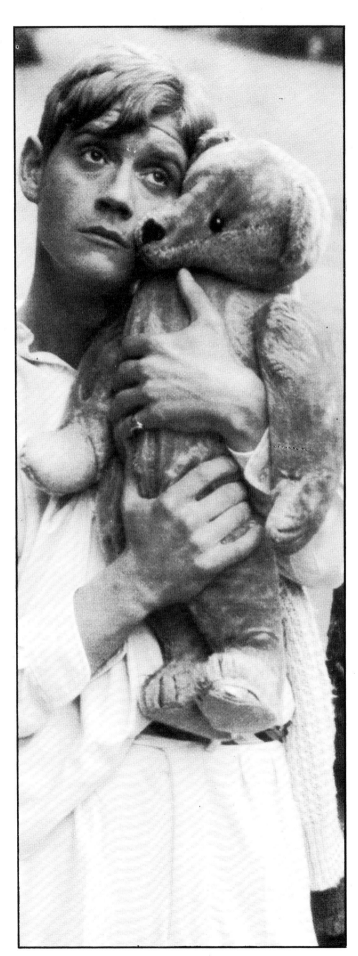

MY TEDDY BEAR

Written to Commemorate the Teddy Bear's
Seventy-Fifth Birthday

He sits upon his pillowed throne
A joyous smile upon his face.
And though his ears may seem outgrown
He carries them with pride and grace.

He's never cross or quick to carp
A friend in need is he to me.
When human tongues are mean and sharp
My Teddy gives me sympathy.

To him I always bare my soul
He lifts me when I'm feeling low.
And when I brag and miss my goal
He never says, 'I told you so'.

My friends may titter gleefully
And some may tease, but I don't care.
I hope that I will never be
Too old to love my Teddy Bear.

JEFFREY S. FORMAN
The New York Times October 27 1977.

"A really bad day at the office, Charles?"

(LEFT) *Anthony Andrews with one of the bears from Peter Bull's collection in a scene from Granada Television's production* Brideshead Revisited *by Evelyn Waugh. Anthony plays Lord Sebastian Flyte and the teddy is his permanent companion named 'Aloysius'*
(ABOVE) *Cartoon by Bill Maul for* The Rotarian, *1979.*
(FACING PAGE) *A little arctophile and a huge hug of teddies in East Anglia.*

INTRODUCTION
The world of Arctophiles

THIS is a book for *arctophiles*.

In case the word is new to you—which it may well be—and you're wondering if it applies to you—which it almost certainly does as you've picked up this book—then let us explain further.

The word *arctophile* is derived from the Greek *arktos* meaning bear and *philos*, friend. So if you own a Teddy Bear, collect them or just find them irresistible then you're part of a world-wide fellowship enjoying the hobby of *Arctophily*. As a lover of bears—for the term embraces model bears of all kinds, not just Teddy Bears—you can consider yourself an *arctophilist* and feel welcome to this celebration of the little creature that has been called the world's most popular stuffed toy. Who says so? None other than that prestigious organisation, the National Geographical Society, who announced in a report published in November 1974:

'Throughout the world there will soon be Teddy Bears lying in wait beneath Christmas trees ready to conquer youngster's hearts. Over the years they may have been better at it than any other Christmas toys. Countless ancestors of this year's Teddy Bears have been killed with kindness, smothered with love that may cost them a chewed ear, or unbuttoned eye, or wrenched shoulder seam. The Teddy Bear is the King of Stuffed Bears and all other toys.'

Although as an adult you may still have in your possession some inseparable, ragged old Teddy much loved from the days of your childhood, or, as a child, have just discovered the unique fascination of one of these furry creatures, it will probably come as something of a surprise to be told that there is already in existence a whole underground army of *arctophiles* spread around the world. An army of all ages, and growing bigger all the time. What, in fact, has happened is that now the secret is out. Teddy Bear lovers are everywhere—and proud of the fact!

Listen to what journalist Vickie Mackenzie wrote in the Australian magazine, *Women's Weekly*, in April 1979: 'Do you love your Teddy Bear? Do you carry him

you cuddle good...

One of a delightful series of Teddy Bear cards produced by the Harlequin Gallery in America.
(BELOW) Daily Express *cartoon, October 3 1979.*

'During the first half of the Twentieth Century it was found that the subtle appeal of the Teddy Bear was so endearing and enduring that the Teddy has become the lasting symbol of childhood, and consequently outlived all other mascot animals. It is now realised that anybody who thinks the Teddy Bear is just a cuddly toy and nothing more is very much mistaken. There is far more to Teddy than meets the eye. For there is now ample evidence to show that the Teddy Bear gives solace and enjoyment to people of all ages and both sexes. So much so, in fact, that this takes it right out of the classification of a soft toy.'

But these are deep waters which must be explored in their own good time. The purpose of this book is much broader—to explain, illustrate and celebrate the impact of the Teddy Bear on all of us. And if you have any reason to think we might be over-stating the case, let's look at some facts and figures.

Since the creation of the first Teddy Bear in the early years of this century (he's actually a real newcomer to the world of toys, you see)★ his popularity has grown to such an extent that it is estimated that the annual world figure for the sale of Teddy Bears is in excess of £30 million, and may well be getting nearer £50 million by the minute. (It's $40 million dollars every year in America alone at the moment!) That represents an almost incalculable number of large and small, thin and fat, furry and cuddly, dressed and undressed, brown, black, white, multi-coloured and multi-featured Teddy Bears pouring from almost every nation on the face of the earth.

The number of Teddies of all ages still in existence must indeed be legion. For Teddy Bears do not die, only love and affection causes them to wear away. People just don't part with them like other toys—nor do they very often sell them, which accounts for the rarity and collectability of the older types.

If we may illustrate the point further, in 1972 it was reported that in the United Kingdom alone 63.8% of all households contained one or more Teddy Bears, and that there was a statistically significant relationship between their popularity and the number of children in the household. And according to *Bear Tracks*, the

★ *The earliest carved figures of dancing bears which may have been used as toys can be traced back to the Sixteenth Century, but actual models of bears go back much further than this. The oldest examples still in existence are from China and date from the Chan Dynasty (1122–722 B.C.) and Han Dynasty (206 B.C.–A.D. 220).*

around with you, talk to him secretly, cuddle him when you're feeling down? Are you 45? Be not ashamed. The day of the *arctophile* liberation is at hand. . . . The world is full of them. Millions of grown-ups treasure their battered, eyeless, one-eared, furry little friends. The closet doors are about to spring open (as they did for women and gays a little earlier) and *arctophiles* will pour forth.'

What's more there is far more significance to being 'Teddy Bear Conscious'—that is aware of their importance in your life—than you may have realised.

Colonel Bob Henderson, one of the leading experts on Teddy Bears, and a man who has played a considerable part in the creation of this book and not surprisingly features extensively in it, puts the matter into focus for us (he will develop the theory in detail later in the book):

TRAMPS by Iain Reid drawn by Fiddy

MAYBE WE COULD SELL TED...

WHAT?

HONEST, TED... HE WAS ONLY TEASING!

newsletter produced by James T. Ownby, 'It has been estimated that there must be at least 170 million Teddy Bear fans and 500 million Teddy Bears in the United States alone.' (We'd better be careful what we say about them from hereon—just imagine what would happen if all that lot took offence at mankind!)

This infiltration by the Teddy Bear into our lives has been very subtle, achieved almost without most of us being aware of the fact. And it is only when you sit down and take stock of how widely he features in everyday life that some idea of the extent of his influence emerges.

There is a whole library of books about fictional Teddies, of course, and he's been featuring in films, television, and on radio not to mention in newspapers, magazines, comics and in advertising pretty consistently over the past three quarters of a century. He's had songs written about him, poetry composed in his honour and his likeness has appealed to numerous artists and cartoonists. For year's he's been one of the most popular characters on birthday and post cards. Teddies have raised fortunes for charities, been promotional free gifts, appeared as the showpieces of exhibitions, and delighted thousands of all ages at rallies, picnics and all manner of fund raising activities. He has his own clubs, has been featured on many foodstuffs, and just about any household item you care to name. He has been a lucky mascot at more types of sporting events than any other stuffed toy—and will be again in 1980 as Mishka, the symbol for the Olympic Games in Moscow. He has his own hospitals, of course, and has even been the subject of several medical papers, including one on his own ailments grandly entitled, 'Some Observations on the Diseases of *Brunus edwardii* (Species nova)' published in 1972. And on top of all this he's broken enough records to deserve his own edition of the *Guinness Book of Records!*

Most of all, though, he's given comfort and solace to

Teddy featured on stamps to mark the 'Year of the Child' and (BELOW) *appearing on the front covers of magazines as different as* Investor's Chronicle *and* Woman's Weekly!

children in both sickness and health, and been a companion to the lonely, the disadvantaged and the elderly. Even as we write there is news of him taking on a new dimension as the inspirer of hard-pressed business people. In America, two talking Teddy Bears are being offered for sale to executives and their ladies. The bears for men in their pin-stripe suits, white shirts and red ties, repeat in a gruff voice, 'You're on your way to the top—you're a born leader!' while those for the woman in white skirts and vests with red striped blouses announce in a gentler tone, 'Be what you want to be. You're perfect, just perfect. Ms. Bear says you're a winner!' Over half a million of them have already been sold, apparently. (Incidentally, we liked the comment about these bears by Patricia Boxall in her column in the London *Sunday People* of June 17, 1979: 'The day will surely come when somebody's Teddy is going to square up to somebody else's Teddy and tell them what they should do with their boss!')

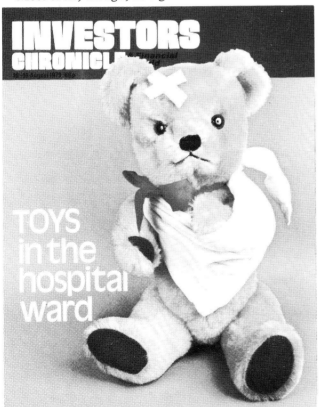

The fascinating treatise on the illnesses of teddies by D. K. Blackmore, D. G. Owen and C. M. Young published in The Veterinary Record, *1972.* (BELOW) *The favourite wine of teddies and their owners—over 16, of course!*

While on the subject of Teddy Bears giving support to business people, we should perhaps just note that Britain's first woman Prime Minister, Mrs. Margaret Thatcher, owes a debt of gratitude to one. For during her successful campaign to win control of the British Parliament for her party, she took with her as a good luck mascot a cuddly version of Paddington the Bear! (Mrs. Thatcher is only one of many people in the public eye who have cause to be grateful to Teddies as you will see going through this book.) Teddy has also been used with great effect to make the tragic children of the refugee

Boat People from Vietnam feel welcome when groups of them have been flown into Britain to begin new lives here.

It all underlines the view that Teddy Bears have the power to exert a great deal of good on humanity, an opinion well expressed by Jim Ownby, the American who started the most famous of the Teddy Bear clubs, 'Good Bears of the World'. A little while back when we were collecting material for this book he said, 'Teddy Bear power is not only love for children and seniors, but for anyone who can appreciate the ideas we have for "Good Bears of the World".'

The ideals of this organisation for doing good work among the sick and the aged through the medium of Teddy Bears seems to negate the often heard suggestion that Teddies are childish. As Peter Bull, another well-known champion of the little bear has retorted sharply, 'Childish? They are no more childish than collecting wives, cars or yachts.'

Not for nothing, then, has this book been called 'In Praise of Teddy Bears'. For the history, development and world-wide appeal of the bear—plus the whole host of personal stories about him and those fortunate enough to be his owners—make for an absolutely fascinating and engrossing story.

At least we, the *arctophiles*, and our millions upon millions of furry little friends think so. . . .

PHILIPPA AND PETER WARING

Good Bear Day, 1979.

Portraits of two famous bears. (LEFT) 'Gilbert' who lives with Yvonne Langley in Woollahra, Australia, and 'Teddy Girl' the remarkable bear belonging to Colonel Bob Henderson of Edinburgh, Scotland.

(TOP LEFT) *Illustration from a Twelfth Century bestiary of the belief that a bear licked her cubs into shape.* (BELOW) *Brown Bear and Polar Bear.* (RIGHT) *Black Bear and Grizzly Bear.* (FACING PAGE, TOP) *Restored head of a Short-faced Bear,* Arctotherium bonoerense, *looking decidedly Teddy Bear-like!* (BOTTOM) *A couple of delightful Pandas and a Koala.*

THE TEDDY BEAR'S ANCESTORS

THE bear is an older inhabitant of the Earth than man himself, and its great longevity has undoubtedly contributed to it achieving a special place in folk-lore, myth and legend. Bear-like creatures roamed the world more then twelve million years ago, but it was not until something like one million years ago that the true bear appeared and was later named *Ursus* (the Latin for bear) to differentiate it from its predecessors.

Perhaps not surprisingly, the bear came to be worshipped by early man, and evidence has been found that Neanderthal man had a bear cult which elevated the giant cave bear of 75,000 years ago into a god. With the passage of time legends developed about bear gods and goddesses, and such stories are particularly prevalent among the North American Indians. One of the most widespread mythical ideas about bears was that their young were born as formless lumps which the mother bear then licked into the shape of tiny cubs. (They are actually very small, blind and hairless at birth.) This belief gave rise to the expression of a child being 'licked into shape' by its parents.

Our modern bears fall into four main types, all belonging to the Plantigrade tribe, so called because they walk on the whole sole of the foot, in contrast to the Digitigrades, such as dogs and cats, who rest their weight only upon the toes or front part of the paws. Bears are found in nearly all parts of the world (with the exception of Australia which is the home of their relative, the koala) and it is a well known fact that they never willingly attack human beings. These are the four main types:

Polar Bear (*Thalarctos maritimus*) is found in the North Arctic regions only and is one of the most handsome creatures in creation. It is the largest of all the bears, rarely smaller than eight feet in length and sometimes as much as eleven feet, and covered with beautiful yellowish-white fur. The Polar bear is a great swimmer, very agile in the water, and can cover distances of up to forty miles at a stretch.

Grizzly Bear (*Ursus horribilis*) from the American continent is next in size to the Polar bear, but surpasses it in strength and ferocity. Its fur varies in colour from light grey to blackish-brown, and the creature got its name 'Grizzly' from the fact that this fur is either tipped with grey or shot through with grey hairs giving it a grizzled effect.

Black Bear (*Ursus Americanus*) is also a dweller of the American continent, but much smaller than the Grizzly—usually about five feet long—and has smooth,

black, glossy hair. The bear will attack small quadrupeds, but lives chiefly on berries and roots, although its great delight is eating honey and it will brave repeated stings to secure a honeycomb!

Brown Bear (*Ursus arctos*) is found over much of the world, in particular Europe, Russia, Asia and even Japan. It's hair is usually brown, but it can vary from almost black to virtually yellow. A solitary animal by nature, it has a rather good-humoured appearance created by its large eyes and pleasing expression. It can, though, hug its enemies to death in its strong embrace!

It should be mentioned that the bear family is related to the raccoon (*Procyonidae*) to which the Panda family (*Ailurus fulgens*) also belongs. The largest member of this group is the much admired Giant Panda (*Ailuropoda melanoleucia*). Here again *uro* like *arcto* means bear-like, and in China where the creature lives it is called 'beishung' meaning 'the white bear' and models of it are regarded as Teddy Bears. Likewise the koala from Australia is named *Phascolarctos cinereous*, the *arctos* being included because it is bear-like. In Australia it is called the 'tree bear' or native sloth, and models of it are referred to as 'The Australian Teddy Bear'.

Bears have, of course, featured in romance and literature for centuries, and have a special place in the folk-lore of several nations, in particular Russia—where they are seen as almost man-like because of the way they walk upright. In many Russian stories the bear is usually depicted as 'friendly, hospitable, cheery, the best of comrades, the worst of officials, tolerant of all social

(BELOW) Early version of the story of The Three Bears *by 'G.N.' published in London in 1841, with a wood engraving by B. Hart.*
(RIGHT) Turn of the century picture by L. Leslie Brooke for the same story.

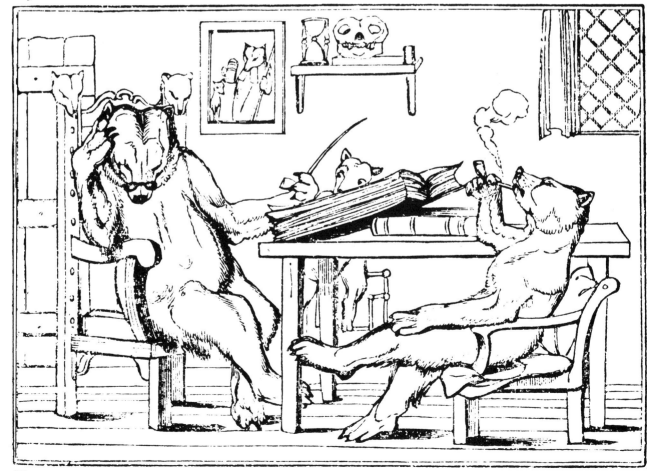

16

МУЖИК И МЕДВЕДЬ

vices, pitiless only to the pretentious', to quote Jane Harrison and Hope Mirrless in their *Book of the Bear* (1926).

For many people the most famous of bear stories is *The Three Bears*, widely believed to have been an old fable first written down by the English writer, Robert Southey in his miscellany, *The Doctor*, published between 1834 and 1847. In fact, there is an earlier manuscript version of the story written by a lady named Eleanor Mure at least three years earlier than Southey. The work, bearing the title 'The Celebrated Nursery Tale of The Three Bears; put into verse and embellished with drawings for a Birthday Present to Horace Broke, September 26, 1831' now resides in the Osbourne Collection of Early Children's Books housed in the Toronto Public Library. What is particularly interesting about the mysterious Mrs. Mure's version (for we know absolutely nothing about her) is that it is an old woman and not a young girl who steals the bears' porridge and then falls asleep in their house. She also gives the tale an ending not found elsewhere in which the bears discover the old woman and then punish her in a most heartless way:

> '*On the fire they throw her, but burn her they couldn't,*
> *In the water they put her, but drown there she wouldn't;*
> *They seize her before all the wondering people,*
> *And chuck her aloft on St. Paul's church-yard steeple;*
> *And if she's still there when you earnestly look,*
> *You will see her quite plainly—my dear little Horbrook!*'

Of other famous stories about bears which appeared before the advent of the Teddy Bear, we should perhaps just mention the delightful tales about Bre'r Bear in the Uncle Remus books written by the American, Joel Chandler Harris, in the closing years of the last century. They in particular served as a most appropriate way of heralding the birth a few years later of the Teddy Bear— in effect the descendant of all these bears we have just discussed.

(ABOVE) *Russia's famous bear, Mishka, from a collection of Russian folk tales, 1963.*
(BELOW) '*Brer B'ar' in a spot of trouble with a Bull-frog from* Uncle Remus *by Joel Chandler Harris, illustrated by J. A. Shepherd, 1902.*

17

DRAWING
THE LINE
IN MISSISSIPPI

Berryman 1902

THE FATHER OF THE TEDDY BEAR

T HE man we have to be most grateful to for our little friend the Teddy Bear is none other than a former President of the United States of America, Theodore Roosevelt, who was born in 1858 and died in 1919. He was the twenty-sixth man to hold that great office and as the many biographies about him have shown, he was a larger-than-life figure much loved by the people of America.

Theodore Roosevelt was actually of rugged Dutch and Scottish ancestry, and although born in New York, he quickly grew to love the great outdoors of America. While still in his teens he became a skilled rider, a crack-shot huntsman, and a bold explorer. But his life was dedicated to public service, and in 1884 he became leader of the New York legislature. Later appointments saw him hold the office of President of the New York Police Board and Assistant Secretary to the US Navy.

His name came to widespread public attention in 1898 when he raised and commanded a group of men known as 'Roosevelt's Rough Riders' who fought in the Cuban War. This activity enabled him to draw on all the

(FACING PAGE) *The famous cartoon by Clifford Berryman which lead to the creation of the Teddy Bear.* (ABOVE) *Another Berryman cartoon of Roosevelt's bear hunt.* (BELOW) *President Roosevelt photographed on a bear hunt at the time of the famous 'Teddy's Bear Incident'.*

backwoods lore he had learned as a young man and his was a fighting force to be reckoned with by the enemy.

On his return to America, Theodore Roosevelt was made Governor of New York State and then in 1901 he became the Republican Vice-President. That same year, following the tragic assassination of the incumbent President, William McKinley, he assumed the highest office in the land.

In the years which followed, though he was always kept busy and hard at work, Roosevelt liked to take the occasional breaks from statesmanship and relax by recapturing the pleasures of his youth hunting with groups of friends. His great passion was for hunting bears, in particular grizzlys, or if they were not to be found, the more common black and brown bears. But the President was not solely interested in killing them as he explained in his book, *Outdoor Pastimes of an American Hunter* published in 1905:

'Frequently I have been able to watch bears for some time while myself unobserved. With other game I have very often done this even when within close range, not wishing to kill creatures needlessly, or without a good object; but with bears, my experience has been that chances to secure them come so seldom as to make it very distinctly worth while improving any that do come, and I have not spent much time watching any bear unless he was in a place where I could not get at him, or else was so close at hand that I was not afraid of his getting away.

'On one occasion the bear was hard at work digging up squirrel or gopher caches on the side of a pine-clad hill;

while at this work he looked rather like a big badger. On two other occasions the bear was fussing around a carcass preparatory to burying it. On these occasions I was very close, and it was extremely interesting to note the grotesque, half-human movements, and giant, awkward strength of the great beast. He would twist the carcass around with the utmost ease, sometimes taking it in his teeth and dragging it, at other times grasping it in his forepaws and half-lifting, half shoving it. Once the bear lost his grip and rolled over during the course of some movement, and this made him angry, and he struck the carcass a savage whack, just as a pettish child will strike a table against which it has knocked itself.

'At another time I watched a black bear some distance off getting his breakfast under stumps and stones. He was very active, turning the log or stone over, and then thrusting his muzzle into the empty space to gobble up the small creatures below, before they recovered from their surprise and the sudden inflow of light. From under one log he got a chipmunk, and danced hither and thither with even more agility than awkwardness, slapping at the chipmunk with his paw while it zigzagged about, until finally he scooped it into his mouth.'

President Roosevelt found the habits of grizzly bears particularly interesting, he said, and noticed their variations of temper. 'There are savage and cowardly bears', he wrote, 'just as there are big and little ones; and sometimes these variations are very marked among bears of the same district, and at other times all the bears of one district will seem to have a common code of behaviour which differs utterly from that of the bears of another district'.

Although the President was a brave and skillful hunter, he did have one close shave with a bear which he described in his autobiography written in 1913:

'The only narrow escape I met with was from a grizzly bear. It was about 24 years ago. I had wounded the bear just at sunset, in a wood of lodgepole pines, and, following him, I wounded him again, as he stood on the other side of a thicket. He then charged through the brush, coming with such speed and with such an irregular gait that, try as I would, I was not able to get the sight of my rifle on the brain-pan, though I hit him very hard with both the remaining barrels of my magazine Winchester.

'After my last shot, the first thing I saw was the bear's left paw as he struck at me, so close that I made a quick movement to one side. He was, however, practically already dead, and after another jump, and while in the very act of trying to turn to come at me, he collapsed like a shot rabbit.'

It was on the afternoon of November 14, 1902, however, that the incident occurred which gave birth to our little friend, the Teddy Bear.

A small bear of the kind President Roosevelt refused to shoot. (RIGHT) Two sketches made by President Roosevelt for his children of an amusing incident that happened on one of his hunts: 'The Bear Plays Dead' and 'The Bear Sits Up'.
(FACING PAGE) *Illustration by Eleanor Mure for her very first version of the story of* The Three Bears *drawn in 1831. And Smokey Bear, the character allegedly created as a result of President Roosevelt's bear hunt, and now used in the campaign to prevent forest fires.*

President Roosevelt was visiting the South that month. He had made the journey to settle a boundary dispute which had arisen between Mississippi and Louisiana, and planned to draw a new line between the two States to settle the matter. During a break in the negotiations, he was invited to go on a special hunting expedition which had been arranged for him at Smedes on the Mississippi Delta. The organisers of the trip were well-meaning folk and were naturally anxious that their special guest should be assured of shooting at least one bear. When none materialised during the normal course of the hunt, a frantic search was begun to find one.

Unfortunately all the searchers could locate was one small bear cub which they drove towards the position where the President was standing, rifle in hand. The great man took one look at the sad little creature and turned his back. He 'drew the line' at killing anything so small.

There is, however, another version of this incident which has recently been put forward, and which ought to be mentioned here. According to Gregory C. Wilson of Massachusetts, a devoted researcher of both Theodore RosseveIt and the Teddy Bear, the bear which the President refused to shoot was not a cub, but a full-grown animal. In an article, 'The Birth of the Teddy Bear' in the Fall 1979 issue of the American, *Bear Tracks* magazine, he describes the day of the hunt and the fruitless search for a bear, in particular the efforts of one of the local guides, who he names as Holt Collier.

'By early afternoon', writes Mr. Wilson, 'T.R. felt Collier must have lost track of the bear so they returned to camp. Soon after they returned, they heard Collier's horn indicating a bear was at bay. They ran to the spot where they found Collier had a huge 230 pound bear entangled with ropes and surrounded by dogs. It was an old bear and lame in one foot. Several people shouted, 'Let the President shoot the bear', but the embarrassed T.R. would not take a trophy in such an unsportsmanlike manner. Indicating he would not shoot the bear, he insisted they stop tormenting the animal. John Parker (who later became Governor of Louisiana) requested permission to kill the animal with his hunting

knife and T.R. agreed. The bear was killed, skinned and packed for the Smithsonian Museum. On the way back to camp, the three Associated Press newsmen allowed on the hunt wrote stories which were sent across the country.'

But to return to the more widely quoted story of the bear having been a cub. According to one later account the cub was found on its own because it had been deserted by its mother. As it is most unusual for a mother bear to leave a cub, it is further believed the little animal may have fallen from a tree or, more likely, that it had fled from a forest fire and thus become separated from its parent. One persistent legend maintains that the cub's fur was actually singed and that this is one of the main reasons why the Department of Agriculture adopted the bear as the symbol for their campaign to try and prevent forest fires and also called the character, 'Smokey the Bear'.

In any event, President Roosevelt did not enjoy the encounter and later confided his feelings in a letter to a friend, Philip Stewart, dated November 24, 1902:

'I have just had a most unsatisfactory experience on a bear hunt in Mississippi. There were plenty of bears, and if I had gone alone or with one companion, I would have gotten one or two. But my kind hosts, with the best of intentions, insisted upon turning the affair into a cross between a hunt and a picnic, which always results in failure for the hunt and usually in failure for the picnic. On this occasion, as a picnic it was pleasant enough, but as a hunt simply exasperating, and I never got a shot. Naturally the comic press jumped at the failure and have done a good deal of laughing over it!'

This might well have been the end of the matter if one of the most famous cartoonists of the day had not heard of the incident and immortalised it in the cartoon shown on page 18. The double-meaning of the sketch is underlined by its caption, 'Drawing the line in Mississippi!' The cartoonist's name was Clifford K. Berryman of the *Washington Evening Star* and after its initial appearance on November 18, the drawing was soon being republished all over America. (As a matter of interest, Clifford Berryman's daughter has added a little more detail to the shooting incident. Writing to a correspondent recently she said, 'Every time I heard father tell this story, he concluded by saying that when Roosevelt saw the tiny cub he said, "If I shot that little fellow, I couldn't look my own children in the face".')

Mr. Gregory Wilson, in his article 'The Birth of the Teddy Bear' has a slightly different interpretation to put on the double-meaning of the cartoon's caption. He says that Berryman's reference to Roosevelt 'drawing the line' was an unsubtle pun on the 'colour line' as the President was then a strong supporter of civil rights for America's black people and was getting much hostility towards his views in the South. Mr. Wilson writes, 'The cartoon clearly showed T.R. would not shoot "black bears" brought to him on ropes. It graphically portrayed T.R.'s unyielding support of black civil rights.' Mr. Wilson closes his fascinating but controversial report with the statement, 'Thus, the Teddy Bear was born as a result of a racial pun.'

What does remain beyond dispute is that neither the President nor Clifford Berryman could have possibly realised that they had played crucial parts in 'creating' the Teddy Bear.

(LEFT) '*Teddy in Timberland*' *one of many American cartoons to feature President Roosevelt with a Teddy Bear, drawn by C. A. Macauley, 1907.*
(FACING PAGE) *President Roosevelt's great grandchild, Susan, with the original 'Teddy's Bear'.*

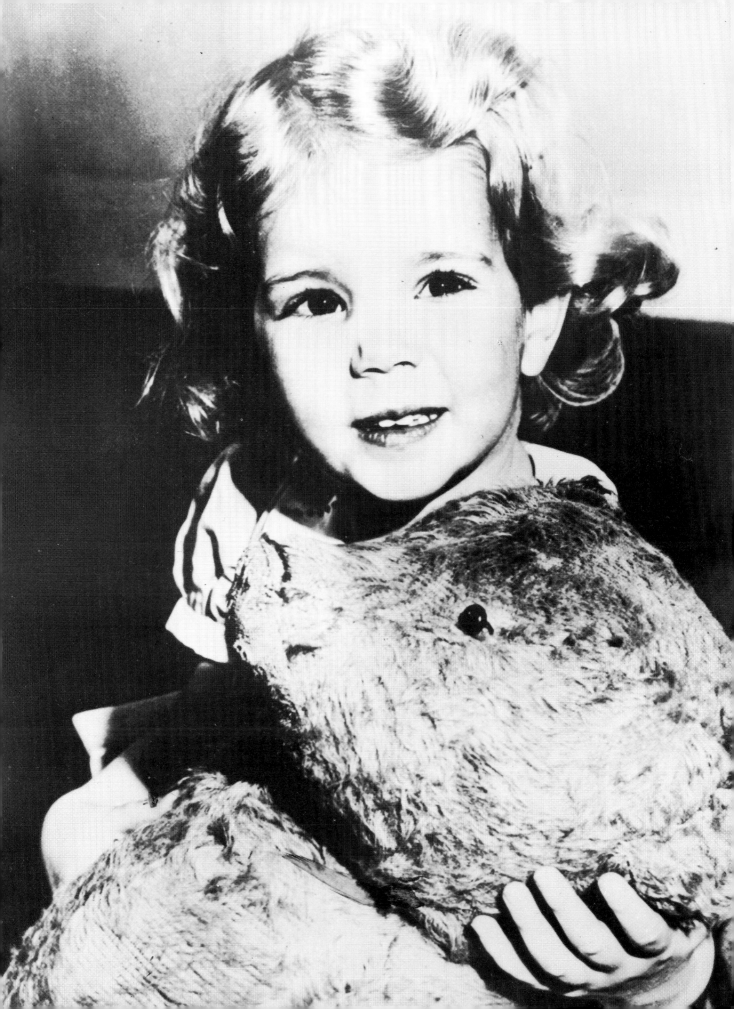

WHO MADE THE FIRST TEDDY BEAR?

ONE of the most surprising facts in the story of the Teddy Bear is that it is almost impossible to say who made the very first one! Indeed, the very first bear-like cuddly toys were created at virtually the same time quite unbeknown to one another on the opposite sides of the Atlantic!

If we are being exact about the term 'Teddy Bear', then the earliest example was certainly made by an American, but there is also no disputing that a German manufacturer made a cuddly toy bear at the self-same time. And without wishing to throw further confusion into the debate, it has to be stated that the Russians, with their long tradition of love for the bear, had been making replicas of the creature in everything from fur to wood for centuries beforehand! However, in this book we are primarily concerned with the Teddy Bear so let us consider the American and German claims as being of greatest importance.

It is perhaps not altogether surprising that it was a Russian immigrant to the United States who made the first Teddy Bear. The man's name was Morris Michtom and his mind was steeped in the traditions from the old country: he had even had wooden replicas of bears among his childhood toys. He well appreciated the symbolism of the bear was as deeply rooted in the consciousness of the nation as that of the eagle in America and the bulldog in Britain, and knew many of the stories about Russia's most famous bear, Mishka, hero of a hundred folk tales.

At the crucial moment in our story, however, he was running a small candy store in the Brooklyn district of New York.

Mr. Michtom was a hard-working, intelligent man always trying to anticipate the new interests among his customers and thereby increase his business. Both he and his wife were clever with their hands, and frequently made dolls and other small playthings to sell alongside the sweets and confectionery. He was well aware how children needed dolls and animal toys to whom they could confide their troubles.

And it was when Morris Michtom saw Clifford Berryman's cartoon of 'Teddy Roosevelt's Bear' in November 1902 that he had the idea which was to make him famous. He decided he would create a toy replica of the delightful little bear that the kind-hearted President could not bring himself to shoot.

To make his bear, Mr. Michtom took some brown plush which he thought the nearest in appearance to the real creature's fur. This he cut into the shape of a bear cub, stuffed it, and added movable limbs and button eyes. The result was an appealing little creature who seemed to be just begging to be loved.

(FACING PAGE) Morris Michtom and a model of one of 'Teddy's Bears'. Margarete Steiff and a replica of her original bear 'Friend Petz'. (ABOVE) Richard Steiff who produced the sketches for the first German toy bears based on his observations in the bear pit at Stuttgart.

Unsure what the reactions might be, Mr. Michtom put his new creation in the window of his shop. On one side was a copy of the Berryman cartoon and on the other a notice which proclaimed the toy to be 'Teddy's Bear'. Five minutes later the shopkeeper had his dilemma resolved when a customer walked in and asked to buy the bear. And by the end of the day he had orders for a dozen more of the bears.

But the dramatic success of his 'Teddy's Bear' also presented Mr. Michtom with a problem. He knew he really ought to have the President's permission to market the toy under his name.

Rather nervously, the Brooklyn shopkeeper made up a special bear and posted it off to the White House with a letter explaining what he had done and asking whether the President would mind his name being used in this context. Mr. Michtom waited apprehensively for the reply, sensing that if the answer was no, his good idea would be ruined.

If the answer had been *no*, of course, our little friend the Teddy Bear might never have come into existence.

When a letter did arrive from Washington, Mr. Michtom tore the envelope open with shaking hands. Inside was a brief note in the President's own handwriting. The shopkeeper's heart jumped for joy at what he read.

'Dear Mr. Michtom', the reply said, 'I don't think my name is likely to be worth much in the toy bear business, but you are welcome to use it'.

With the President's approval, Mr. Michtom prepared to develop his production of 'Teddy's Bears'. And by the following year he was manufacturing them by the hundreds and had established himself as the Ideal Novelty and Toy Company. In 1907 the company became a corporation and today it is one of the biggest toy manufacturers in America.

(TOP) *Two Steiff models of what the company call the 'Original Teddy'.*
(ABOVE) *Three pre-First World War Teddies, all have humped backs and shoe-button eyes. Also a miniature bear sent as a souvenir from Yellowstone Park in the 1920's.*
(FACING PAGE) *Steiff bears over the years—and also the variations in the company's famous* knopf im ohr *'button in ear' symbol.*

Because in 1903 it was impossible to patent a trade name it was not long before others were copying Mr. Michtom's success and before the new century was a decade old, there were at least a dozen other Teddy Bear manufacturers in America: one, based in Chicago, was even called the Theodore Bear Company!

When Morris Michtom died in 1938 his family received a letter of condolence from President Roosevelt's widow and newspapers throughout the nation mourned the passing of 'The Teddy Bear Man'.

The story of the other person who began making toy bears at this same time takes us across the Atlantic to Germany, another nation with a long tradition of making outstanding children's toys. The central figure in this episode is a remarkable young woman named Margarete Steiff, the daughter of a Master Builder, who was born in 1847 in Giengen-an-der-Brenz, Wurtemberg in the picturesque Black Forest region.

Unhappily, tragedy struck Margarete when she was only two years old—she contracted polio which left both her legs paralysed and she had to spend the rest of her life in a wheel chair. But by all account she was not a person to let her infirmity spoil her life, nor restrict her energetic mind, and as she grew to maturity she found she possessed great skill in the parts of her body not affected by the polio, her hands, and she quickly became an accomplished seamstress. (She and her sister in fact owned the first hand-driven sewing machine in Giengen.) Although she herself never married, Margarete developed a great love for children, and when small friends came to visit her she took to making them small animals out of the remnants of cloth she had left over from dressmaking, her primary vocation. The first of these toy animals was a felt elephant made in 1880.

Initially, she gave the little figures away, but soon more of her acquaintances, both young and old, began wanting the elephants. According to the Steiff family records, Margarete made eight of them in 1880, by 1885 she had made 596, and the following year over 5,000. In 1886 a monkey was added to the line, followed by a donkey, horse, pig and camel. To fulfil the demand, the young seamstress naturally had to take on members of her family as well as local women to help her.

By the close of the century, Margarete was producing a whole range of soft toy animals, and then in 1902, her

1914

1926

1933

1903

1953

1966

1978

eldest nephew, Richard Steiff, who had been employed to create new lines, brought her another idea. It was a toy bear, with movable head and limbs, which he had designed as a result of observing brown bears in the Zoological Gardens in Stuttgart while studying for his degree in art. Initially, apparently, she was not taken with the idea, as the bear was made in fur-like mohair plush which was difficult to obtain and it was larger than traditional toy animals.

But the following year, in 1903, at the annual Leipzig Toy Fair, fate intervened on behalf of the bear. A buyer from an American toy importing agency called at the Steiff stand and said he was having no luck in finding something soft and cuddly for the U.S. market. The family tried without success to interest him in their various lines, and had almost given up hope when they remembered the out-of-favour fluffy bear.

According to the Steiff family legend, the buyer took one look at the little creature and to everyone's surprise promptly placed an order for 3,000 of them!

When the news of the sale was relayed to Margarete Steiff back in her workshop in the Black Forest, she had to admit she had been wrong not to share Richard's belief in the toy. Nevertheless she quickly generated the enthusiasm to fulfil the order—and within months it was clear the toy bear was destined to become Steiff's most successful line. The little chap was named 'Friend Petz'.

During the subsequent year twelve thousand of these bears were exported mostly to America and England. By the year 1907 there were four hundred factory hands and eighteen hundred women working in their homes to keep pace with the orders pouring into Giengen. (According to Steiff records, in 1907 the output reached 974,000 and although this has subsequently proved an all-time peak, in 1953, the golden anniversary of the teddy bear, production was at a steady quarter of a million per year and this figure has remained constant every year since.)

The year 1908 saw the introduction of the 'growler' which caused the Teddy Bear when tilted backwards to make an animal noise in the same way that the 'squeaker' apparatus makes a baby doll cry. Further developments which the Steiffs' introduced were bears that could be dressed up and (when the term Teddy Bear was in common usage) the 'Teddy Bear Baby'. Steiff bears were also made easily distinguishable from all others by having a small button inserted in their ears—the symbol being referred to as *knopf im ohr*.

It is perhaps interesting to note at this juncture that once the term Teddy Bear was universally accepted, the word 'Bruin' which had been used by children for centuries when referring to baby bears disappeared to be replaced by 'Teddy'. Other generally recognised nursery names such as 'Bunny' for rabbit and 'Pussy' for cat have, however, never changed.

Although Margarete Steiff died in May 1909, she had lived long enough to witness the universal acceptance of the Teddy Bear by both girls and boys, and the firm which bears her name still flourishes in Giengen today. In local parlance it is not surprisingly often called 'The Teddy Bear Town'.

Looked at in hindsight, it is perhaps fair to say that while it was Morris Michtom who created and named the Teddy Bear as we know it today, it was Margarete Steiff who popularised it and started the world-wide craze for bears. There can surely be no denying it became a phenomenon during both their lifetimes far beyond anything they could have imagined.

But to return to our history. In his book, *Children's Toys Throughout The Ages* (1953), Leslie Daiken has some interesting things to tell us about what was happening in Britain during those early days:

'While this toy drama was unfolding in the Black Forest, the idea occurred to British makers that, since the plush used in the German bears came from Yorkshire, it would be feasible to manufacture Teddies

in Britain. In order to compete with cheap labour abroad, the shape was modified. The long, thin Teddy was being made on the principle of the German soft dolls of the period, which consisted of a large bag for the body and four long thin sacks for each limb. The English makers radically changed this shape by shortening the body, making the limbs better proportioned and giving a

(ABOVE) *A humped-back Teddy with a copy of one of Seymour Eaton's famous Roosevelt Bears books.* (BELOW) *Pre-First World War Teddy Bear clothing and another early popular American Teddy Bear book.* (FACING PAGE) *Uncle Sam congratulates his famous 'Bear Ambassadors' Teddy-B and Teddy-G, 'The Roosevelt Bears'.*

(ABOVE, LEFT) *An early German Teddy Bear with 'bag' body and long, thin 'sack' arms.* (RIGHT) *An American bear from which the plush fabric has been completely worn by a great deal of loving!* (BELOW) *Teddy Bear advertisement from the 1907 Sears Roebuck catalogue.*

plumper appearance to the animal. The earliest English bears were filled with kapok, a soft, resilient, natural material grown mostly in Indonesia. The head was enlarged and filled with wood-wool, a type of wood shavings of a finer quality than that used for packing of wooden cases. A new method was perfected for joining the limbs which insured a tight fit to the body. All wires that might injure a young child were left out. This method of fixing is a closely guarded secret among the manufacturers of Teddy Bears to this day. Toys in which growlers are inserted must be hand-filled with wood-wool, as kapok, being soft and fluffy, would enter the holes of the voice-box, and prevent the growl from functioning.'

The speed with which the world's children took to the Teddy Bear was nothing short of amazing, and soon the little creatures were making friends all round the globe—and of all ages, too. It has been argued in some quarters that the reason for the Teddy Bear's success was that it came onto the market at a time when there was a great need for a toy for boys, dolls being considered unsuitable for them. Just as dolls appealed to the feminine and maternal instincts in girls, so the toy bears apppealed to the masculine, hunting and parental instincts in boys. What really happened, of course, was that both sexes found the little creatures absolutely irresistible!

"TEDDY BEARS" ARE ALL THE RAGE.

The Best Plaything Ever Invented.

THESE BEARS ARE THE MOST SENSIBLE AND SERVICEABLE

toys ever put before the public. Not a fad or campaign article, but something which has to stay on merit alone. An article which will afford your children and even yourself much enjoyment and lasting pleasure. Made of the finest quality imported bear plush they resemble the little cubs. They are full jointed and will assume countless different positions, all of which we illustrate. Each bear has a natural voice produced by a soft pressure on front of body, and they are practically unbreakable. We offer these bears in a natural cinnamon color only. The larger the size the better proportioned and more nearly the order one of these bears at once for your boy or girl, and you will find that the toy which you could select would give them more actual pleasure and

No.	Size		Ship'g W't	Price
18H23358	10 inches high	9 ounces		$0 75
18H23360	12 inches high	11 ounces		1 15
18H23362	14 inches high	14 ounces		1 73
	16 inches high	18 ounces		2 38

In a remarkably short space of time it was quite clear that something more than just a toy had been created: the Teddy Bear became recognised as a symbol of love and affection that exerted a fascination for adults, too. This popularity was fully evident by 1908 when the bears were being mass produced on both sides of the Atlantic, and the Steiff factory alone made almost a million of them that year! Today, as the output worldwide shows no sign of decreasing, it is probably fair to say that the Teddy Bear's appeal has outlived and outlasted all other mascot animals.

What subsequently became known as 'The Teddy Bear Fad' in America really began in the year 1906. It then became fashionable to have a Teddy Bear on the side lamps of your car, and one of the first direct spin-offs, an iron money box called 'Teddy and the Bear Bank' was manufactured by the J & E Stevens Company of Connecticut. The first advertisements for the toys also began to appear in the toy trade magazine, *Playthings*, and the earliest located in the May issue reads:

THIS IS BRUIN'S DAY!

The American Line of Jointed Plush Bears is the *Real Thing!*

*Polar Bear **Cinnamon Bear ***Grizzly Bear

Baker & Bigler, Sole Manufacturers
77-9 Bleaker Street, corner of Broadway,
New York City

Another advertisement of the same time placed by a firm called Kahn & Mossbacher declared: 'Make our happiest hit your happiest hit ... everything for the Teddy girl and Teddy boy.' An advertisement from a company called Ferguson showed a Teddy Bear in a baseball suit, another in overalls and a third in a Rough Rider uniform. Toymakers Selchow & Righter promoted the 'Roosevelt Bears' printed in colour on 16 × 18 inch sheets—the sections to be cut out and made up to resemble the regular plush bears. The same company also had a game called 'Hunting With Roosevelt'.

Strangely, the first time the term 'Teddy Bear' was actually used in an advertisement in *Playthings* was not until the September 1906 issue when a small panel by the E. I. Horsman company proclaimed:

Imported Teddy Bears

Best quality, with voice $4.50 to $72 a dozen;
also domestic Teddy Bears with voice,
Horseman's extra quality $9 to $36 a dozen.

The craze for Teddy Bears soon reached such a pitch that doll manufacturers began to fear their sales would be adversely affected, and it required a leader in *Playthings* to allay their worries. 'A Teddy Bear', the Editor wrote, 'is a toy, and a doll is a doll, and every little girl wants a doll, and the fact that she wants a bear will not diminish that desire'.

In a fascinating article, 'Teddy's Bear' in the American antiques magazine, *Spinning Wheel* (April

1971), Emma Stiles says of the Teddy Bear Craze at this time, 'The Teddy Bears were not only a toy for youngsters, aged one to ten. They became collectors' items for teenagers of both sexes who lavished as much affection on them as the little tots did. The unparalleled furore of Teddy Bears worried a number of people. Editorials began to appear in journals scorning women who carried Teddy Bears about with them. A Michigan priest denounced the Teddy Bear as "destroying all instincts of motherhood and leading to race suicide". Within four years of Teddy's introduction to the toy world, almost every child had one.'

Miss Stiles also says that the craze became so widespread that manufacturers were making every conceivable kind of toy carrying the Teddy Bear name. She explains: 'There were Teddy Bear pails, tea sets, carts and cages; there were puzzles and games. Teddy Bear stationery came on the market. There were Teddy Bear muzzles, leashes, squeeze balls, hammocks, postcards, candy boxes, favors, party games, balloons, shooflies, rocking horses, books, card games, pins, rubber stamps, water pistols, scarfs, banks, blocks, wagons, targets and paper dolls, even Teddy Bear briefcases made of plush. Pedal cars were advertised with bears driving them. Strauss, the toy king, made a self-whistling Teddy Bear. There were boats made to fit any bear. A tumbling bear was made, and a bear with a doll's face. The craze kept on and on. Teddy Bears were everywhere. . . .'

Unlike many crazes, however, this one did not die out when President Roosevelt left office. Many of the spin-offs certainly disappeared, but the demand for Teddies themselves went on constantly. Those that got lost were quickly replaced, and any that were almost loved to death were carefully repaired. Durability became the bear's middle name.

Although President Roosevelt was kept busy with the affairs of government while all this was going on, he was certainly not unaware of the success being enjoyed by the little creatures bearing his name. Increasingly, too, he was associated with the Teddy Bear in political cartoons (a typical example is reproduced on page 22) and, not surprisingly, he turned this to good advantage by using one as a campaign symbol when he ran for re-election in both 1904 and 1912.

An interesting story is also told of his visit to England in 1905 when he made a trip to Cambridge University. There a group of students dangled a Teddy Bear on a piece of string from an upper window just as he was passing by. Without the slightest show of embarrassment the great man halted, took hold of his namesake and solemnly shook his hand! In America he doubtless heard the most popular of corny jokes about him: 'If Theodore is President of America with his clothes on, what is he with them off?'—'Teddy Bare!'

One can only wonder today what the reaction of this remarkable man might be to the fact that his most enduring fame is not as a statesman, or as a reformer, or even as a hunter. But for giving his name to perhaps the most popular and beloved of all soft toys.

PAWNOTE: A claim has also been advanced that the Teddy Bear got its name from Edward VII, who, as the Prince of Wales, visited the London Zoo in 1880 and took a particular fancy to a small Australian koala bear which had recently arrived. Although the koala is known in Australia as the Teddy Bear, there is no evidence to suggest this visit gave rise to the term—all the more so because the koala is quite different in appearance from the first toy bears that were made.

Steiff Fiftieth Anniversary Catalogue (1953) and Ideal Toy Corporation 75th Anniversary booklet (1978).

On the following pages are a selection of R. K. Culver's distinctive
illustrations for the stories of the Roosevelt bears. Above, they are
setting out on their travels across the Atlantic. Their paw marks were
also featured in each book! On the facing page, Teddy-B and Teddy-G
are shown in a jaunting cart in Ireland and in a perilous position up the
Eiffel Tower!

TEDDY-G—His paw

TEDDY-B—His paw

THE ADVENTURES OF THE ROOSEVELT BEARS

With some details of Teddy Bright-Eyes
The Human Teddy Bear!

THE Teddy Bear craze which began in 1906 created a public demand for all manner of related items as we have seen in the previous section. And although books about the new character did not appear quite as swiftly as many of the other *objets d'art*, those which came onto the market were in time to become valuable and eagerly sought after by collectors. Of these the most popular and now most coveted were the adventures of two characters known as Teddy-B and Teddy-G, 'The Roosevelt Bears' created by a man named Seymour Eaton.

These two spirited and ingenious bears admittedly looked rather more like real bears than Teddies, but the source of their inspiration was obvious and they found immediate acceptance among readers when their adventures, in pictures and rhyming verse, began to appear in newspapers across America. From 1905 onwards, young and old alike awaited impatiently for each day's newspaper to follow the latest rollicking episode about the two bears. For a year the adventures were syndicated through twenty newspapers, and then the first of four books compiled from the serial appeared.

The initial title in the series was *The Roosevelt Bears— Their Travels and Adventures* which ran to 180 pages with both black and white and coloured illustrations by V. Floyd Campbell. The lively verses which accompanied the pictures described the bears' experiences as they travelled by train from their home in the Rocky Mountains to New York. The second book, *More About The Roosevelt Bears* (1906) continued the bears' adventures in New York and described their return journey to Colorado including a meeting with their namesake on

the way! The illustrations in this volume were by R. K. Culver and followed the style established by Floyd Campbell.

The third book, arguably the best, was *The Roosevelt Bears Abroad* (1907) and was again illustrated by R. K. Culver. This took the bears across the Atlantic to Britain (where they met King Edward), through Europe and then home by way of Egypt. The final book in the series was *The Bear Detectives* (1908) in which Seymour Eaton described how Teddy-B and Teddy-G solved several mysteries relating to a number of nursery characters including the whereabouts of the tails belonging to Little Bo-Peep's sheep! The illustrations for this volume were by Francis P. Wightman and William K. Sweeney.

Collectors of these books have sometimes been surprised to come across smaller volumes of adventures of the two bears. These editions had fewer coloured plates and sold for 40 cents instead of the $1.50 asked for the first four titles. The books were in fact published

33

about the time of the First World War and were actually segments taken from the original four volumes hence their titles which included, *The Adventures of the Travelling Bears, The Travelling Bears in New York, The Travelling Bears in Out-Door Sports, The Travelling Bears Across the Sea, The Travelling Bears in England* and so on. Though easier to find than the original four, these reprint volumes are nonetheless eagerly sought after and fetch quite high prices.

In an interesting article 'Teddy Bear Fever' in *Spinning Wheel* (June 1972), Julie and Linda Masterson have written, 'In popularity, Teddy Bear stories were only second to the Teddy Bear itself, and none were in greater demand than those written by Seymour Eaton.' However, they go on, 'this admiration for Teddy-B and Teddy-G was not shared by everyone. Educators and librarians unanimously agreed the stories lacked literary merit, but then Seymour Eaton never claimed any for his stories. He repeatedly stated, "The story is simply a

The Roosevelt Bears in London. (BELOW) *The bears meet King Edward and are highly complemented.* (FACING PAGE) *Up to high jinks in the Tower of London.*

"We'll make steel fly and sabres clash,
And burst this old tower all to smash."

good, wholesome yarn, arranged in a merry jingle and fitted to the love of incident and adventure which is evident in every healthy child".'

Seymour Eaton claimed to have based his stories on acts of mischief committed by children he knew, and this may well have caused libraries in particular to refuse to stock his titles—a fate that was also suffered by another contemporary writer later to enjoy world-wide fame, L. Frank Baum author of *The Wizard of Oz*. Despite his undoubted popularity, no place has been found for Eaton in any of the standard reference books on children's writers of this period.

Julie and Linda Masterson add some further information on the elusive Eaton: 'Because many critics treated Seymour Eaton harshly and claimed he was an opportunist who made money by promoting sales through the use of a famous name, he frequently felt the

Teddy-B enjoying a stein of beer during the Roosevelt Bears's visit to Germany, and Teddy-G trying his hand as a serenader in Venice.

need to justify his position. In press releases, as well as in the preface to *The Travelling Bears*, he stated: "Since the name Roosevelt has been used in the story it may be of public interest to know that President Roosevelt and his boys have been pleased with the story as it appeared in serial form".'

What also seems evident is that Eaton had a very high opinion of his work for in 1908 he said, 'Children's favourites come and go, but there are a few, like Red Riding Hood, Cinderella, Silverlocks, Aladdin and Jack the Giant Killer which go on forever. The Teddy Bears are now in this class . . . Teddy-B and Teddy-G have earned the dominating position which they occupy. No other nursery character ever had such a popular following.'

Such apparent arrogance naturally did not endear him to some people, and they were no doubt secretly pleased when the popularity of the two bears declined sharply during the years of the First World War. The new generation of children wanted stories rather than jingles and verse, and while the old nursery favourites continued to exert their magic, Teddy-B and Teddy-G who their author had presumptiously placed among them, disappeared from the shelves. Even the framed coloured pictures, chinaware, glass plates, and jug and pitcher sets which had been manufactured with the bears' likenesses on them no longer appeared in the shops.

One of the mysteries that has persisted about Teddy-B and Teddy-G to this day is what their initials stand for. It has been suggested that they are Teddy-Bad and Teddy-Good, though the respective bears do not show such characteristics exclusively. For a time there was an idea that the letters were used to distinguish between bears designated as boys or girls, because of the highly advertised line of 'Teddy Boy and Teddy Girl Clothes' made by the firm of Kahn & Mossbacher at the time of

Two of the earliest British books to feature Teddy Bears. The anonymous Tale of Teddy Brighteyes *published in 1909, and* Tim Tubby Toes *by Harry Golding, illustrated by M. M. Rudge, 1914.*

The Roosevelt Bears run into trouble in Russia and find themselves thrown into prison.

the great Teddy Bear 'fad'. In fact the answer is much simpler than this, and is to be found on page eleven of *The Travelling Bears*, today the hardest of all the Seymour Eaton titles to find. The significant lines read:

> The black bear's name was Teddy-B;
> The B for black or brown, you see.
> And Teddy-G was the gray bear's name;
> The G for gray; but both bears came
> For 'Teddy' because everywhere
> Children called them Teddy Bears.
>
> The 'Teddy' part is a name they found
> On hat and tree and leggins round,
> On belt and boot and plates of tin,
> And scraps of paper and biscuits thin,
> And other things a hunter dropped
> At a mountain camp where he had stopped.
>
> And how some boys, the stories tell
> Liked these two Teddy Bears so well
> That they made a million for the stores to sell;
> Some quite little, for children small,
> And some as big as the bears are tall;
> The brown ones looking like Teddy-B.
> And the white as funny as Teddy-G.

Although it is possible that some copies of the Roosevelt Bears' books found their way across the

All ends happily for the Roosevelt Bears. After a stop-over in Egypt, Teddy-B and Teddy-G return to America by way of Canada.

Atlantic to Britain, it was not until 1909 that the first English book to feature a Teddy Bear appeared. Entitled *The Tale of Teddy Bright-Eyes* it is the story of a naughty little boy who is punished by being turned into a living Teddy Bear by 'The Bad Boy's Fairy' Lady Thingummyjig. The book describes his adventures trying to get returned to his former self.

No author is credited on the cover or title page of this undoubtedly important work, and all attempts to discover his or her identity have failed. Copies of the book are also of the utmost rarity, and the example quoted from and illustrated here was kindly loaned from the collection of Mrs. Nita Rigden of Canterbury. The book was published by Humphrey Milford of London and printed by Thomas Forman & Sons of Nottingham, but the records of neither firm can throw any light on the author of what can be reliably claimed to be the first British story to feature a Teddy Bear. The volume measures three inches wide by four inches deep, has a four colour cover (reproduced in this book) but is without illustrations inside. The anonymous author's style is rather reminiscent of blank verse as this opening episode will demonstrate:

THE TALE OF TEDDY BRIGHTEYES

'There was once a very naughty boy, he was round and fat and stumpy, the sort that ought to be merry and gay; but he was sulky and grumpy. He was always saying 'Shan't' and 'Won't!' and 'Do as I like' and 'Don't care' as cross as two sticks. And every one called him a Regular Little Bear.

One day he'd been especially bad. He'd been put in the corner once for doing his lessons so badly (he was really a perfect dunce, for he wouldn't take the trouble to learn). He'd been put in the corner twice, for quarrelling with his sisters, to whom he was never nice; so at last his mother sent him out-of-doors in sheer despair; and he spent his time in trying to find how best to be naughty there.

Teddy, for that was his name, to begin with, swung with all his force on the garden gate. This was forbidden—that's why he did it, of course. And as the hinges creaked and squeaked, and bang, bang, bang went the gate, he saw a little old woman coming; she walked at a wonderful rate for one so old. And she said to him, politely, 'I beg your pardon, but could you tell me whereabouts is the little Wee Bear Garden?'

Teddy had not the least idea what she was talking about. He turned his back on her, slammed the gate, and rudely replied, 'Find out!'

Then the old woman grew and grew, and rose up tall and big, and said 'I'm the Bad Boys' Fairy, the Lady Thingummyjig. I've heard you were a regular Bear—I've come for myself to see. And, Master Teddy, a Bear you are, and a Bear you shall henceforth be, till you find the Little Wee Bear Garden, and that you won't do just yet, I promise you, you shall be very sorry that ever you met with me today. But you've got one chance. If ever you really need help at once—if ever you feel you're very repentant indeed for all your horrid crossness—break off a hawthorn twig and call aloud, Come, B.B.F.! Come, Lady Thingummyjig.' And the tall old woman disappeared.

Well, Teddy, as you may suppose, was all in a tremble and twitter, down from his head to his toes. 'What could she mean?' he said at first: and then, 'It can't be true! I shall not turn to a Teddy Bear! Of course not; people never do.'

But as he spoke, he felt uncomfortable because he saw his hands, before his eyes, were changing into paws! He felt his face in alarm and haste—it was covered with furry hair! 'My goodness me!' said Teddy. 'I *have* turned into a Teddy Bear!'

He ran indoors to his mother—you know, its the only place is a mother's knee, whenever one's in trouble or disgrace—and she shrieked with fear when she saw him. 'Oh, mother dear!' he exclaimed, a terrible thing has happened—I do feel so ashamed.'

And he told her all about it: and then he asked, 'Is it true? Do I really look like a regular Little Bear to you?' His mother was too upset to

other boys and girls about the Lady Thingummyjig. You shan't be called a Bear again, for that would be a shame. For the future, Teddy Bright-Eyes shall be your nice little name. For happy hearts make sparkling eyes, and you shall be happy now! Goodbye, my dear!' and she vanished.

I hardly need to tell you how rejoiced the mother of Teddy was, when she saw this wonderful change that had come upon him. As everything was so exceedingly strange, she said, 'It's no good wondering why things have happened like this. I've got you back, my darling!' and she gave him a hug and a kiss. 'Mother, as long as I'm with you again', said Teddy, 'that's all *I* care'.

'And never, never again, shall I be a regular Little Teddy Bear!'

Another story, delivering much the same moral lesson and in a similar format as *The Tale of Teddy Bright-Eyes*, appeared a year later, but featured a bear rather than a Teddy Bear. This was *A Bad Little Bear* and again there was no author mentioned, although the illustrations are credited to E. Aris and the publishers are given as Henry Frowde. The book tells the story of a naughty little bear who steals a honeycomb and is punished by the bees.

Tim Tubby Toes who followed four years later in 1914 was also passionately fond of honey, but when he stole several jars and ate them all he felt so sick he had to be given a large spoonful of castor oil and packed off to bed! The story was told by Harry Golding with illustrations by M. M. Rudge. The book was one of a series of 'Little Wonder Books' published by Ward, Lock & Co Ltd just prior to the First World War.

The format of *Tim Tubby Toes* was identical to that of the Beatrix Potter books published by Frederick Warne of London, and Warne's also introduced a bear at this period who delighted younger readers. *Mrs. Bear* was one of the characters who appeared in a series of 'Mr' and 'Mrs' books (not to be confused with the modern 'Mr. Men' books by Roger Hargreaves), all of which were illustrated by the talented Lawson Wood whose work is now much coveted by collectors. So popular did Mrs. Bear become that she was even featured in advertising for Iron Jelloids tonic pills!

Although there were certainly other books around at this time which featured bears, the important Teddy Bear characters did not begin to emerge until after the end of the First World War, and such is their importance that they are to be accorded separate entries in the next section.

speak—but she took him by the paw and led him to the looking-glass, and there indeed he saw a regular Little Teddy Bear. And there indeed his last hope ended. The worst of it was, he couldn't see how matters could be mended. As for his mother, she loved him, in spite of the trouble and care he had brought upon her. She cried, and kissed her unfortunate Little Bear.

Of course, the plight of the Little-Boy-Teddy-Bear soon attracts sightseers who begin to hang around the house, and also newspaper photographers anxious to try and take a picture of him. In despair he runs away to try and find the Wee Bear's Garden. During his journey he falls asleep and a little girl drags him home thinking he is a giant sized Teddy Bear! The girl's father turns out to be a doctor and gives the boy some help before he continues on his way. At the climax of the story, Teddy is captured by two men who make him perform as a dancing bear, and in his fright he finally calls for Lady Thingummyjig promising that he will never again misbehave. The tale ends:

Then Lady Thingummyjig stooped down, and to his immense surprise, she kissed him, with a lovely smile, and beautiful shining eyes. And she said, 'Look round about you!' and behold! he instantly found he was standing under a notice that said, 'The Wee Bear Garden Ground'. Scores and scores of good little Teddy Bears were scampering to and fro—there were swings and ponds with model yachts, and wonderful flowers a-blow, and hoops, and cricket, and skipping-ropes, and everything you can need to make you very happy and very contented indeed. 'You see what a jolly place it is!' said she, 'all full of joy; now, will you stay as a little Bear, or go home as a little boy?' 'Oh, please, go home!' said Teddy. Then she replied, 'I'll take you there straight away!'

He found himself in the Fairy's arms, at home, inside the gate. She kissed him on the eyes and chin, and said, 'When you grow big, tell the

(ABOVE) *Another unique early British Teddy Bear story,* Bibble, Bobble and Bubble *written and illustrated by a child authoress, Josephine Hatcher, and published in the 1920's.*
(RIGHT) *The fate of* A Bad Little Bear, *an anonymous work with pictures by Henry Frowde, circa 1910.*

AN A~Z OF SOME FAMOUS BEARS

Four children's favourites: Rupert (British), Smokey (American),
Billy Bluegum (Australian) and Bussi Bar (German).

ALBERT

(Great Britain, b. 1968)

In just over ten years, Albert the little Cockney bear from London's East end has become a tremendous children's favourite. His creator, Alison Jezard, originally wanted to write some stories about a kind of Winnie-the-Pooh figure brought up to date and getting involved in adventures in contemporary situations—in fact she has created a unique character who has become instantly recognisable in his cloth cap, thanks considerably to Margaret Gordon's excellent pictures. Albert is a very friendly bear who lives at the delightful address of 14, Spoonbasher's Row, not far from his great friend, Henry the junk-cart horse. His other particular pals who feature in his adventures are his cousin Angus from Scotland, Tum-Tum the Panda, and the robust Digger the koala.

ANDY PANDY'S TEDDY

(Great Britain, b. 1951)

Andy Pandy's Teddy was the first Teddy Bear to become a television star. Andy himself is a little clown, but a clever one, and it is poor Teddy who invariably gets into trouble or does something silly. Andy Pandy first appeared on British television in the programme 'Watch with Mother' in 1950, but it was not until the following year that Teddy made his bow. The films featuring Andy, Teddy and their other friend, Looby Loo, a rag doll, have been widely shown abroad (particularly in Australia and New Zealand) and more recently stories about the trio have been appearing in children's comics. With almost 30 years of appearing on the small screen behind them, Andy and Teddy are still among the most popular characters with younger viewers.

BIG TEDDY & LITTLE TEDDY

(Great Britain, b. 1916)

Big Teddy and Little Teddy were an inseparable pair who appeared in stories written by Mrs. H. C. Craddock in the years between the two World Wars and were as popular with young readers then as Paddington and Rupert are today. The large, gruff Big Teddy with his little friend who was missing an arm and a leg were two of the toys who belonged to a small girl called Josephine and they, perhaps more than any of the others, were the cause of any mischief or naughtiness that occurred in the stories. Mrs. Craddock is believed to have based her books on the toys and Teddy Bears owned by her own daughter, Margaret, and no doubt their popularity was helped considerably by the many attractive and colourful illustrations by Honor C. Appleton which appeared in the twelve Josephine books. Little Teddy also has the distinction of being the only important Teddy Bear character in literature to have some of his limbs missing!

BILLY BLUEGUM

(Australia, b. 1904)

Billy Bluegum an irascible and highly amusing koala bear is by far the most famous and popular cartoon animal in Australian history. Ever since the brilliant Norman Lindsay first featured him in a sketch in the Sydney weekly publication, *The Bulletin*, in August 1904, he has risen to become a national hero. (As a matter of interest, Billy did not actually receive his name in Lindsay's illustrations until January 1908.) Billy's adventures which mirrored Australia's own social developments during the first half of this century also appeared in *The Lone Hand*, a monthly magazine published by the same company as *The Bulletin*, and on occasions Norman Lindsay used him in political drawings and allowed him to be used in advertising campaigns. Although Lindsay died in 1969, his work has now become highly valued among collectors, and new generations of Australians are enjoying Billy Bluegum through republication of some of his adventures in book form.

BIMBO

(Spain, b. 1965)

Spain's favourite Teddy Bear is to be found in shops and supermarkets from one end of the country to the other. He's a delightful little chap called 'Bimbo' who is featured on a whole range of bread and cakes, and he and the products bearing (oops!) his name have been popular with the Spanish people as well as tourists for a good many years now. Anyone who has tasted his wares will agree he's a dab hand at baking!

BUSSI BAR

(Germany, b. 1969)

In just ten years, Bussi Bär has firmly established himself as the favourite Teddy Bear with German children and his magazine is one of the best selling juvenile publications in the country. Bussi, with his captivating, wide-eyed expression, and faithful friend, Bello, a little blue dog, enjoys all manner of exciting adventures which are retold and drawn by their creator, the talented cartoonist, Rolf Kauka. 'The Friends of Bussi Bär', as his readers are known, run into many thousands.

CORDUROY

(United States, b. 1968)

In less than ten years, little Corduroy has found himself a place in the hearts of many American children and has recently crossed the Atlantic to earn the same kind of affection in Britain. Don Freeman, Corduroy's creator, retells his adventures with great charm, from the moment a little black girl's mother refuses to buy him because he is missing a button on one of the straps of his overalls. Naturally upset, Corduroy sets out to find another button, having to overcome a number of dangers in the huge department store where he lives, but although he has no luck, the little girl unexpectedly returns the following day to buy him after all!

THE GRETZ TEDDY BEARS

(United States, b. 1968)

The five Teddy Bears created by Susanna Gretz are almost childlike in their characteristics, and they all live together in a modern house with a large Dalmatian dog called Fred. The Bears, named William, Andrew, Charles, Robert and John, are each different colours and vary in temperament from William who is always dreaming of his next meal to Charles the scholar who is always deep in a book. Apart from her own books, Susanna Gretz also illustrates the series of stories about a little bear called Rug which are written by Helen Cresswell.

TEDDY EDWARD

(Great Britain, b. 1962)

Teddy Edward is remarkable among famous Teddy Bears in that his adventures are all told in photographs, taken by Patrick Matthews who, with his wife, Mollie, relates the stories. The original Teddy Edward who first appeared in books in 1962, was a Teddy Bear who belonged to Mr. and Mrs. Matthews's daughter, Sarah, but the bear in use today is actually a rather younger fellow who had to go to the Hammersmith Doll's Hospital for some 'Fur Surgery' to make him the double of his predecessor! Teddy Edward is now the star of his own series of television films which are shown in the 'Watch With Mother' programme, and this has involved him in considerable travel to such exotic locations as Spain, Greece, India, Nepal, Bermuda and even the Sahara Desert.

MARY PLAIN

(Great Britain, b. 1930)

Mary Plain is a delightful and mischievous little bear whose first adventure, *Mostly Mary* appeared in 1930. Of the thirteen subsequent books written by the author Gwynedd Rae, it is pleasing to note that over half are still available. Miss Rae got her idea for Mary Plain while visiting the famous Bear Pits in Berne, Switzerland, and indeed the first book, *Mostly Mary*, is made up of incidents she actually observed there. In the stories which followed, Mary showed herself to be something of a character as capable of getting into trouble as of pulling off some splendid act of rescue, being very brave into the bargain. Aside from solving problems and mysteries, she lent a hand in the war effort (*Mary Plain in Wartime*, 1942) travelled extensively (*Mary Plain Goes to America*, 1957, perhaps the best of the books) and earned her place as a literary celebrity (*Mary V.I.P.*, 1961). All her adventures have been illustrated by Irene Williamson.

MISHKA

(Russia, b. circa Twelfth Century)

The bear has been a favourite in Russian folklore and legends for many centuries and his most common name is Mishka. Performing bears are also a staple in Russian circuses, and at the present time the most popular sweet with the country's children is a 'Mishka'. Over the years, Mishka has been depicted by a whole host of talented artists and it is only possible to show a fraction of their work here. A Teddy Bear called Mishka is the subject of a cartoon series, and in recent years his adventures have taken him into space as an astronaut, emulating the achievements of the Russian spacemen! A rather striking Mishka has also been designed by the Russians to serve as the mascot for the Olympic Games being held in Moscow in 1980.

MR. BEAR

(Japan, b. 1968)

Mr. Bear is Japan's favourite bear and his adventures related by Chizuko Kuratomi have been delighting Japanese children for over a decade. Recently the stories, complete with Kozo Kakimoto's highly individual illustrations have been translated into English and gained a strong following among British and American children. Mr. Bear lives in Rabbit Town, but his size dwarfs most of the other inhabitants and he has a knack of getting into trouble however well-meaning his intentions are. Teddy Bear toys as such are not as popular in Japan as they are in Europe and America, but those which are manufactured possess a high degree of individuality like the 'Worker Bear' shown earlier.

NOUNOURS

(France, b. 19th Century)

Nounours is the name of a bear character who has appeared in French newspapers and comics for a number of years, and recently made his debut on television. Although he is ostensibly a bear, he is also a very clever storyteller and has the power to fly whenever he finds himself in a tricky situation! Stories about bears are few and far between in France, and unlike most other countries, French children prefer to call their fluffy toy bears 'Martin' rather than Teddy Bear. Alexandre Dumas' story 'Tom: An Adventure of a Bear in Paris' is still perhaps the most popular French tale of one of these creatures.

ODD

(Great Britain, b. 1971)

The adventures of the little Teddy Bear Odd told in seven books by James Roose-Evans concern his search for the Great Bear. According to legend this Great Bear was present at the Court of King Arthur and has been sleeping in Bear Mountain somewhere in Wales ever since the great king died. The legend says the Great Bear will be awoken by another bear to whom he will reveal the whereabouts of the Lost Treasure of Wales. Odd comes to believe he may be this bear and sets off on his exciting and fascinating quest, accompanied by his friend, Elsewhere, a circus clown. James Roose-Evans the author of this imaginative saga has been a teacher, actor and writer, and based the stories on a little teddy bear and a toy clown in his possession.

PADDINGTON

(Great Britain, b. 1956)

Paddington, perhaps more than any other bear in this A–Z, has enjoyed an absolutely meteoric rise to fame—his adventures are today translated into 20 languages and he appears on television not only in Britain and America, but in France, Germany, Holland, Greece and down under in Australia and New Zealand. According to the books by Michael Bond, Paddington was found sitting on Paddington Station in London (hence his name) after a journey from Darkest Peru and with a label attached to him reading, 'Please Look After This Bear. Thank You.' Actually Mr. Bond got the idea for him on Christmas Eve 1956 when he was trying to find some last minute Christmas presents in Selfridge's store in London. He saw a Teddy Bear sitting all by itself on a shelf. 'I thought the bear looked so lonely that I bought him as a Christmas present for my wife', says Mr. Bond. Ten days later the new arrival had inspired him to write a story—but it still took two years and five publishers before anyone saw the potential in Paddington. 'He's not a cuddly bear', Mr. Bond says of his creation who he thinks has some of his own characteristics (in particular a love of marmalade and old duffle coats). 'He's a bear for standing up in the corner. That's why he wears Wellington boots.' Paddington has now been the subject of eleven books and has celebrated his 21st Anniversary—though he still remains resolutely nine years old, says Mr. Bond! Paddington is unique among literary bears as a double record holder (see the section 'The Teddies' Book of Records') and probably few other types of Teddy Bear sell over one hundred thousand models of themselves each year. Although Paddington has been drawn by innumerable artists for the enormous range of items of merchandise on which he appears, the first and original drawings of him by Peggy Fortnum remain the favourites with his admirers.

PIERRE PANDA

(United States, b. 1977)

Pierre Panda is certainly one of the world's most travelled bears for he is a character created by Pan American Airlines to be used on books and travels aids for youngsters flying on their aeroplanes all over the world. A jolly and appealing little bear, he is a master of entertainment and features in books of quizzes, puzzles and brain-teasers. Pierre is currently the only famous Panda Bear character.

Little Lost Bear. By MARY TOURTEL

. No. 1.—Mrs. Bear sends her little son Rupert to market.

Two jolly bears once lived in a wood;
Their little son lived there too.
One day his mother sent him off
The marketing to do.

She wanted honey, fruit, and eggs,
And told him not to stray,
For many things might happen to
Small bears who lost the way.

ADVENTURE SERIES No. 20

RUPERT

AND THE WILD GOOSE CHASE

In Full Colour including RUPERT and the GLOWING POOL

RUPERT

(Great Britain, b. 1920)

Rupert the Bear is arguably one of the most famous cartoon bears in the world and his adventures have been appearing in the British *Daily Express* since 1920 and have also been published in at least 18 other languages. The stories of the little bear and his friends from the village of Nutwood were first created by Mary Tourtel, the wife of the *Express's* night editor. Rupert's initial purpose was to be a rival to the *Daily Mail's* then popular cartoon character, 'Teddy Tail' who had been delighting children since 1915. Mary, an accomplished sketch artist, was also something of a larger-than-life character having been an aviator and adventurer, breaking air speed records prior to the famous Amy Johnson. She had already published several children's books featuring comic animals and verse, and decided to employ a similar style for her new character designated 'Little Lost Bear'. Following his first appearance in the *Express* on November 8, 1920, Rupert was soon joined by his friends, Bill Badger, Algy, Edward Trunk, Podgy Pig and the Wise Old Goat—who at one time was the most popular character in the strip! In a short space of time Rupert had become a national favourite with his own fan club, 'The Rupert League' and in their bibliography of him, *The Rupert Index* (1979), W. O. G. Lofts and Derek J. Adley have with some justification called him 'The Mickey Mouse of Great Britain'. The Rupert success story continued to grow until 1935, when Mary Tourtel was struck with failing eyesight and had to retire. It proved no easy task to find a replacement because of the difficulty of drawing Rupert precisely, and not until after an extensive search was Alfred Bestall found. The son of a Church Minister, Bestall was already providing work for a variety of adult and juvenile publications, and proved an ideal replacement—he continued the strip for the next thirty years until 1965, since when the adventures have been in the hands of a team of artists. The popularity of the little bear has led to his use on all manner of products including children's clothing, furnishing, tableware, toys, jewellery, confectionery and the like—probably only Paddington has endorsed more items! Like Paddington, Rupert has his own television series, and the little bear is also a star of the stage. Lofts and Adley also believe that nearly 100 million Rupert books of all descriptions have been sold in the sixty years since he was created.

SHOE SHOP BEARS

(Great Britain, b. 1962)

The Shoe Shop Bears are a delightful little band of bears who began life in a shoe shop where they were 'adopted' by the shop assistant, Polly. In fact their creator, Margaret J. Baker, got the idea for the stories in January 1962 when she was in a shoe shop in Taunton, Somerset. There she saw three Teddies being used to amuse young customers while they were fitted with shoes, and soon ideas for a series of adventures began to emerge in her mind. Since Mrs. Baker's first book, *The Shoe Shop Bears* (1964) the original trio of fatherly old Threadbare Boots, motherly Slippers and mischievous little Socks, have been joined by Hi-Jinks, a modern nylon bear and Teabag, a small plastic bear, as well as Hannibal a toy elephant rescued from a rubbish dump and Banger, a basset hound. The illustrations for the early books in the series were done by the splendid C. Walter Hodges, who was followed by Daphne Rowles and most recently Leslie Wood.

SMOKEY BEAR

(United States, b. 1953)

Smokey may well be the best known bear in America, and his face and message are certainly known to millions of children and their parents. He is a character used by the Department of Agriculture in their campaign to prevent forest fires. According to legend, it was because the bear which President Roosevelt refused to shoot in 1902 had been singed by a forest fire that the name Smokey was chosen for this character. But what is a fact is that in 1953, the Ideal Toy Co (whose founder, Morris Michtom, had made the first Teddy Bear in America) was granted permission to manufacture Smokey Bear toys and at the same time recruit children into the campaign to prevent forest fires by making every purchaser of the bears a Junior Forest Ranger. This has understandably enormously increased interest in the campaign and in the bear himself. Aside from the cuddly toys, Smokey also features in stickers, posters and comic strips.

STUBBINS

(Great Britain, b. 1935)

Stubbins is a toy bear who lives with a group of other bear friends at Stubbington Manor, the country home of the rather pompous Lord Rushington. Almost koala-like in appearance, these bears drawn by Dorothy Burroughes, feature in a series of books written by Lady Elizabeth Gorrell in the thirties and forties. Among the other characters in the group who tangled with all manner of humans ranging from difficult shopkeepers to Americans billeted at Stubbington Manor during wartime, were Albert, Velvet Trousers, Sleepie, Golden Syrup, Orange Pekoe and the irrepressible little Bitty. The illustration here is from *The Bear Garden* (1945).

SOOTY

(Great Britain, b. 1949)

Sooty, now an internationally-famous figure with a penchant for magic and mischief, starting life as an ordinary glove puppet which entertainer Harry Corbett bought in a toy shop in Blackpool in 1949 as something to be used at children's parties. He called him simply 'Teddy' and used him in a number of his magic tricks. When, a few years later, Mr. Corbett appeared on television with the little bear he was an instant success, and the pair were offered their own show. Sooty's fame was assured when he became the star of a strip cartoon and replicas of him were manufactured by Chad Valley. Sooty got his name because the original glove puppet had little more than a smudge of black for his nose. Over the years he has delighted children with his magic tricks—although in company with his friends, Soo and Sweep, he can also cause more than a little havoc!

TEDDY ROBINSON

(Great Britain, b. 1953)

Teddy Robinson started his life as just an ordinary Teddy Bear until his young owner, Deborah Robinson, took him to school and her teacher immediately gave him the name which is now familiar to his many admirers. It was Deborah's mother, Mrs. Joan G. Robinson, who then decided to write some stories about the little bear and the adventures he had had with her daughter. Although nothing happens to Teddy until Deborah actually takes him somewhere, it is never very long before he is into some scrape or another, and apart from getting lost more than once he has also had a very dramatic encounter in a hospital! A lot of the Teddy Robinson stories are based on real incidents, and it seems almost a miracle that the original bear has survived to this day. He is now apparently much loved by Deborah's own three children!

WINNIE THE POOH

(Great Britain, b. 1926)

No reader needs any introduction to this world-famous bear, claimed by many people to be the most popular of all Teddy Bears. There is no disputing his importance in a book such as this, and in fact he warrants a section all of his own, in which the book critic Robert Pitman recounts the extraordinary story of his creation and the subsequent development of the legends which now surround him. The article, which begins on page 54, was first published in *The Sunday Express* of June 26, 1966.

Mrs BEAR
GOES TO THE FAIR
By Lawson Wood

A bear featured in the 'Mr' and 'Mrs' series of children's books by the talented and under-rated artist, Lawson Wood. Mrs. Bear Goes To The Fair was one of the best titles in the series which appeared in the 1920's and carried advertising on the back covers!

Iron Jelloids

Iron Jelloids
The Great Tonic

THE REAL TRUTH ABOUT WINNIE THE POOH?

by Robert Pitman

A·A·Milne

An article from The Sunday Express, *June 26, 1966.*

ONE day forty-six years ago a pretty young woman went to Harrods and bought a Teddy Bear for her son's first birthday. The bear had an astonishing future in front of it.

At a big luncheon last week held in the bear's honour at the Dorchester, a cheque was presented to the *millionth* child for whom a copy of last October's paperback book about the bear was bought in just the few months since then. A little mental arithmetic will give you some idea of the steady annual value of the bear. The bear has become an industry.

As for the original animal itself, patched and resewn, it lies in a showcase in New York, as revered and honoured as a bust of Henry Ford in Detroit. It is, of course, Winnie the Pooh, the central figure of the stories which the late A. A. Milne wrote about his son, Christopher Robin.

We all know about Christopher Robin and Pooh. Or do we? During the past few weeks I have been investigating the facts about Pooh. It seems to me that, despite all the admiration and publicity, the full story has never been told. It is, I think you may agree, both sad and mystifying.

First, let us look at the accepted accounts of what happened to the toy bear when it was brought home from Harrods. At the time A. A. Milne was 38, and his wife Daphne was some ten years younger. He was a successful playwright, but he was no John Osborne. He was modest, gentle, ever bubbling with a quiet stream of bizarre humour. This humour, we are told, soon began to flow around the fat, furry shape of the Teddy Bear from Harrods.

One day young Christopher Robin came down from the nursery when the actor Nigel Playfair was visiting. In a gruff voice the boy said, 'What a funny man. What a funny red face.' But he denied saying the words himself. He said it was his toy bear, whom he called Pooh, speaking.

Thus Pooh came to life—along with the boy's other toys, a piglet (bought by friends), a stuffed donkey, a tiger. Adult visitors, when invited, would ask, 'I suppose Pooh is going to be there?'

Milne began writing about Pooh. His wife has recalled: 'We were all acting little incidents with Pooh and the nursery animals the whole time . . . we were all quite idiotic about it. The animals had become very important to us.'

Mrs. Milne has described how Christopher Robin would tell his father: 'Come and see me in my bath. And then you can read the latest story to Pooh.' In her words, 'Even when we were working we had fun in a world of special intimacy and utter silliness, laughing at ridiculous jokes and talking in our own special language. Looking back to those days I always see Pooh and the small boy with whom we shared them . . . with his large brown eyes and beautiful corn-coloured hair cut square.'

Yet is this the whole story? In 1952 when A. A. Milne

was lying ill with only two more years to live, a curious thing occurred. His son, Christopher Robin Milne, then 32, wrote in an article entitled, 'Father':

'Strangely enough, although my father wrote so much about me, he did not like children . . . in fact, he had as little to do with children as possible. I was his only child and I lived upstairs in the nursery with my nanny. I saw very little of him. It was my mother who used to come and play in the nursery with me and tell him about the things I thought and did. It was she who provided most of the material for my father's books. . . .'

About the Pooh stories, C. R. Milne declared: 'As far as I can remember I knew nothing of the stories until they were published. Then my nanny used to read them to me. . . .'

Was the son being fair to his father? We know that as he grew older the boy hated the idea of being the Christopher Robin of the stories and being teased at school with, 'Where's your Teddy Bear?'

But, though unfortunately timed, his article made clear that, in his view, his father was a kind and delightful man. A typical moment: Once, wrote C. R. Milne, 'he found me sitting at the lunch table holding a fork upright . . . Instead of saying, "That isn't the correct way to hold a fork", he merely remarked, "I shouldn't do it that way if I were you. If someone fell through the ceiling, they'd fall on to the prongs and that would hurt them!" '

But what *is* the truth about the writing of the immortal Pooh stories? C. R. Milne now runs a small bookshop in the West Country. Having written his article, he has said little about his father or himself and now politely refuses to say anything at all. Instead I have just visited his mother, Daphne Milne, at her flat high above Green Park in Piccadilly.

She explained to me why she has moved from the Sussex home in Ashdown Forest where the Pooh stories are set. It was because she had lost the housekeeper who had been with the family since Pooh was bought. She told me how she first met her husband.

'It was at my coming-out dance when I was 17. My god-father, Owen Seaman, who was editor of *Punch*, asked me if he could bring along one of his writers, A. A. Milne. I had always read and admired A. A. Milne's articles, so I said, "Of course".

'Life was so elegant then. It's the absence of servants that's made all the difference don't you think? My husband took a toy mascot, a dog called Carmen, to look after him in the First World War. He was saved from the Somme by trench fever. He wrote to say that Carmen had found a French germ up the trench and blown it on to him. Four years after that Christopher Robin was born.

'My husband dictated the stories to me. I didn't type or anything, but he needed an audience to react. He would walk to and fro puffing at his pipe while I wrote and laughed.'

I mentioned Christopher Robin's claim that he never heard the stories until they were in book form. 'Really?' said his mother. 'Oh, no. They were part of our lives.'

Copies of the Pooh books in every language line the shelves in Mrs. Milne's exquisite flat. But she is hardly an old lady living in the past. In her seventies she is still decidedly attractive, vivacious, chic, and an active theatregoer.

One thinks of the laughing amateur secretary taking down A. A. Milne's dictation, and one also remembers what he himself says about his writing—namely that it was never sentimental, that all the characters in Pooh are in fact selfish and as tough as nails, that even the little boy in 'Christopher Robin is saying his Prayers' is actually as egocentric and unfettered by morals as any other young animal.

Were these stories written primarily for a child at all? Or were they, in effect, written for the delight of the child's mother? It is an ironic thought.

Perhaps there is a sadness in the Pooh stories, the sense of a dream existence poised uncertainly on the edge of the harsh real world, which has helped to make them immortal.

MILNE INFLUENCES

In his autobiography, *It's Too Late Now* (1943) A. A. Milne says that there were two major influences on him in writing the stories about Winnie the Pooh—apart from the Teddy Bear bought at Harrods. The first was the book *Uncle Remus* which had been read to him as a child by his father: it was a story he never forgot. The second was the writer Rose Fyleman who first encouraged him to write for children and published some of the verses which later became *When We Were Very Young* (1924). In his autobiography, Milne tells an interesting story about this collection: 'One day when Daphne went up to the nursery, Pooh was missing from the dinner table which he always graced. She asked where he was. "Behind the ottoman" replied his owner coldly. "Face downwards. He said he didn't like *When We Were Very Young*." Pooh's jealousy was natural. He could never quite catch up with the verses.' Whether Miss Fyleman played any part in the actual creation of *Winnie the Pooh* it is impossible to say, but prior to the appearance of Milne's famous work in 1926, she had herself written a short story about a Teddy Bear which was published in the London evening newspaper, *The Star*. It is interesting to conject whether Milne had read 'The Vain Teddy' which is reprinted here for the first time. Another fact which is not widely known is that Milne himself wrote a story specifically about a Teddy Bear entitled 'Miss Waterlow in Bed' which was later collected into his rather neglected book of stories, *A Gallery of Children*, published in 1939. This tale complete with the original illustrations by A. H. Watson (strikingly similar in style to those of Ernest Shepard) is also reprinted here by kind permission of the Milne Estate and George G. Harrap & Co Ltd.

The Auction at Pooh Corner

A really authoritative comment on the sale of an
E. H. Shepard original for £1200

Pooh was humming a Good Hum, Such as is Hummed Boastfully to Others.

"*Sotheby, Botheby,*
Tiddely-pom!
The sketch of our picnic
Has sold for a bomb."

"He means twelve hundred pounds," explained Piglet.

"That's peanuts," said Eeyore.

At the mention of peanuts they all blinched and were silent for a minute. Then Pooh recovered his spirits and said:

"I shouldn't be surprised if we all finished up at the Tate."

"We would have been there already," said Eeyore, "if you had learned to say Wham. And Pow. And Aaaaargh."

"Anyway," said Piglet, "our pictures fetch as much as some old paperweights I could mention and some Important Sixteenth Century Arabian Manuscripts I won't mention."

"Here's Christopher Robin, who has been having Education all morning," said Pooh. "He has lots of Brain."

Christopher Robin began to tell them about things like Shifting Trends and Underlying Social Significance and What the Market Will Bear and the Challenge to Pop Art of Nursery Trad.

Piglet soon excused himself and went off to pick daisies.

"You could all have been famous already," said Christopher Robin, "if you hadn't been famous all the time. I suppose it's my fault really."

Pooh began another Hum.

"*Ho-tiddely-ho!*
We haven't a chance.
We haven't got So-
cial significance."

"There's one thing you haven't told us," complained Eeyore. "Who gets the twelve hundred pounds?"

"The Prince of Pudukota, of course," said Pooh.

"There you go. You're making things up again," grumbled Eeyore. Nobody could persuade him that there was a real Prince of Pudukota, who once had an English nanny, and rose to become a Client of Sotheby's.

"Why," asked Eeyore, "does a man who doesn't exist get twelve hundred pounds for a picture he hasn't drawn?"

Christopher Robin said Art was like that.

Meanwhile, Pooh was sprawling on the ground, making the face-you-make-when-a-Hum-gets-stuck, so they left him muttering to himself.

"*Isn't it rum*
When a Hum won't come?
I ought to be rich—so there!
Isn't it funny
How a bear makes money,
But none of it sticks to the bear?"

On February 5 1968 the original of this illustration by E. H. Shepard
fetched £1,200 when it was auctioned at Sotheby's in London. The
drawing had belonged to Prince Pudukota of Madras, India, and the
auctioneers had estimated the picture would fetch about £800—several
hundred pounds below the final figure!

THE VAIN TEDDY

by Rose Fyleman

THERE was once a toy Teddy-bear who belonged to a little girl called Peggy. He was very
big, almost as big as Peggy herself, and I am
sorry to say that he was very vain.

You see, people always said, when they saw him,
'What a beautiful Teddy-bear!'

Peggy thought there was no one like him in the world.
He always wore a blue bow, and she even made a blue
silk cap for him, which he wore on the top of his head. It
really made him look rather ridiculous, but it had a
feather in it, and the vain Teddy thought it suited him
beautifully, though he would have preferred pink.

'Pink is really my colour', he said to himself. 'I wish
Peggy would realize how well I should look in pink.'

He grew more and more conceited every day. The
other toys didn't like him at all. He used to sit in the
corner and never join in their talk. If anyone spoke to
him, he just said 'Yes' or 'No', in a proud voice, and
stared at the ceiling.

But he was punished in the end.

One day Peggy's mother bought a packet of pink dye

for Peggy's Sunday frock (which had faded very badly in
the sun), mixed it in a great big pot, and left it standing
on the kitchen table.

The Teddy-bear was sitting on the window-sill just
over the table.

'How pretty that dye is!' he thought. 'What a lovely
colour! If only my cap were that colour, how handsome I
should look!'

Then he had an idea. 'If I lean over', he thought, 'my
cap will drop in, and then it will get dyed'.

He leaned over.

'Mind! Mind!' sang the canary.

But he took no notice. He leaned over farther and
farther. Suddenly—splash! splash! He had fallen right
into the pot of dye!

You never saw such a comical sight as he was when
they got him out. Pink all over! Peggy still loved him as
much as ever, but his appearance was utterly spoiled.

'What a funny Teddy!' people said now. In time he
got used to it, but he never really got over it. He was
never known to squeak again.

MISS WATERLOW IN BED

by A. A. Milne

THIS is Miss Waterlow in bed.

Mrs Waterlow is kissing her goodnight, and saying:

'God bless you and keep you, my darling darlingest, my sweetheart, my little baby one.'

Miss Waterlow gives a little far-away smile. She is thinking:

'I know a funny thing to think when I'm alone.'

Mrs Waterlow is looking at her as if she could never stop looking, and saying:

'Thank you, and thank you, God, for giving me my darling darlingest, You do understand, don't you, that it doesn't matter what happens to *me*, but oh! don't let anything terrible happen to *her*!'

Miss Waterlow is thinking:

'I shall pretend I'm big as the moon, and nobody can catch me I'm so big. Isn't that funny?'

'Good-night, beloved. Sleep well, my darling darlingest.'

Miss Waterlow is remembering something . . . something very beautiful . . . but it all happened so long ago that she has forgotten the beginning of it before she remembers the end.

'Oh, my lovely, when you look like that you make me want to cry. What are you thinking of, darlingest?'

Miss Waterlow won't tell.

Yet perhaps for a moment Mrs Waterlow has been there, too.

'God bless you, my lovely', she says, and puts out the light.

Miss Waterlow is alone.

Miss Waterlow at this time was one. It is a tremendous age to be, and often she would lie on her back and laugh to think of all the babies who were None. When she was six months old, Mr Waterlow, who was a poet, wrote some verses about her and he slipped them proudly into Mrs Waterlow's hand one evening. Owing to a misunderstanding, they were used to wedge the nursery window, which rattled at night; and though they wedged very delightfully for some time, Mr Waterlow couldn't help feeling a little disappointed. Mrs Waterlow was, of course, as sorry as she could be when she understood what had happened, but it was then too late. As Mr Waterlow said: Once you have bent a piece of poetry, it is never quite the same again. Fortunately for all of us, two lines at the end, torn off so as to make the wedge the right thickness, have survived. They go like this:

She never walks, and she never speaks—
And we've had her for weeks *and* weeks *and* weeks!

Now the truth was that Miss Waterlow could speak if she wanted to, but she had decided to wait until she was quarter-past-one. The reason was that she had such lovely things to remember, *if only she could remember them.* You can't talk *and* think. For a year and a quarter she would just lie on her back and remember . . . and then when she had it all quite clear in her mind, she would tell them all about it. But nobody can speak without practice. So every night, as soon as she was alone, she practised.

She practised now.

'Teddy!' she called.

Down on the floor, at the foot of her bed, Teddy-bear, whose head was nodding on his chest, woke up with a start.

'What is it?' he grumbled.

'Are you asleep, Teddy?'

'I are and I aren't', said Teddy.

'I forght I were, and I weren't', said Miss Waterlow.

'Well, well, what is it?'

'What's a word for a lovely—a lovely—*you* know what I mean—and all of a sudden—only you don't because—what *is* the word, Teddy?'

'Condensedmilk', said Teddy.

'I don't *fink* it is', said Miss Waterlow.

'As near as you can get nowadays'.

Miss Waterlow sighed. She never seemed to get very near.

'Perhaps I shall never tell them', said Miss Waterlow sadly. 'Perhaps they don't have the word.'

'Perhaps they don't', said Teddy. 'It's a funny thing about them', he went on, waking up slightly, 'what a few words they *have* got. Take "condensedmilk" as an example. It does, but it isn't *really*, if you see what I mean. That's why I never talk to 'em now. They don't get any *richness* into their words—they don't get any what I call flavour. There's no *bite*.'

'I want a word—'

'Better go to sleep', said Teddy, his head nodding suddenly again.

'Shan't I ever be able to tell them?' asked Miss Waterlow wistfully.

'Never', said Teddy sleepily. 'They've got the wrong words.'

Miss Waterlow lay there, wrapt in drowsy and enchanted memories of that golden land to which she could never quite return. She would tell them all about it some day . . . but not now . . . not now . . . not now. . . .

She gave a little sigh, and was asleep.

COMICAL TEDDY BEARS

DENIS Gifford, creator of the British television cartoon series 'Quick On The Draw', and President of the Association of Comics Enthusiasts, leafs through the world's largest comic collection to consider the history of Teddy Bears in the strips. This is what he has discovered:

Many a bowl of Honey Puffs must have curdled in their cream that wet Wednesday morning of November the fourteenth, 1979. The dread headline blazed across *The Sun*, a dark spot clouding the Tenth Happy Birthday Week celebrations of Britain's best-selling newspaper. John Hill, ace newshound, reporting: 'Sad news, chums. Biffo the Bear has fallen on grisly times. His bosses on the *Beano* comic decided he is no longer a star—and have suspended him for two months. The long-running adventures of Biffo, once Britain's best-loved cartoon character, have been pushed out (can you bear it?) by Christmas advertising.'

A 'Shock-Horror!' report indeed: but *The Sun* was late with the news. *The Guardian* had broken the story the previous day, but regular readers of *The Beano* had already been without their Biffo for three long weeks. His last dated appearance was on October 27th. Very different treatment from the fanfare that heralded his arrival on the full-colour front page of January 24th, 1948. 'Hip Hurray! Biffo the Bear is Here Today!'

The little black bear in the red button-down pants was the creation of the late Dudley D. Watkins, who has probably been revolving in his Dundee grave since the

2. Well, the Teddy Bears sang and danced, and the audience thought it was very nice, too. And as the Teddy Bears went on with their entertainment they got a bit heavy on their feet, or something, and unluckily —

day they displaced Biffo with Dennis the Menace. It was on September 14th 1974 that this earth-shaking shift occurred, marking the moment in time when British comic heroes switched from our four-legged friends to our two-legged enemies. Funny animals had lost the day and Spotty 'Erberts taken over!

As President of the Association of Comics Enthusiasts, the only club for British comic collectors, I was invited to comment. *The Sun* gave a succinct precis of

(ABOVE) *An early British comic strip featuring a Teddy Bear—'Little Willie Winks and his Toy City' from* The Butterfly.
(BELOW) *A complete episode of 'Bobby and the Woolly Bears' which also appeared in* The Butterfly.

1. Bobby and the Woolly Bears started out one fine morning to go a-fishing. Everything in the garden was lovely, and they all felt as happy as possible.

2. When they reached the stream, one of the Woolly Bears caught a swan. And, our word, how they all laughed! But who's that coming up the back?

3. 'Twas the farmer, and he, being a cantankerous old merchant, kicked all the bears into the river. Nice kind of thing to do, wasn't it? However, Bobby fished them all out—

4. And took them home and pegged them out to dry. Poor little Woolly Bears! Not much of an ending to their day's fishing. Better luck next week!

TEDDY, "THE TERROR" OF JUNGLEVILLE SCHOOL.

The other day a fearful thing happened at Jungleville School—Teddy got hold of a catapult! Of course, he started practice at once—on the boys. "Plenty of peas but no peace," chuckled Teddy, catching Jumbo a terrific stinger on the nose. "How does that feel, Jumbo?" "Not at all nice," wailed the unfortunate pachyderm. "I wish you would stop it at once!"

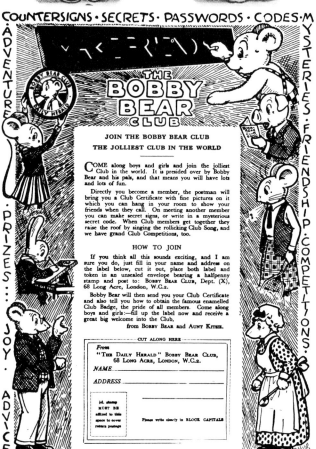

COUNTERSIGNS · SECRETS · PASSWORDS · CODES · MYSTERIES · FRIENDSHIP · COMPETITIONS · JOY · ADVICE

ADVENTURE · PRIZES · JOY · ADVICE

THE BOBBY BEAR CLUB

JOIN THE BOBBY BEAR CLUB
THE JOLLIEST CLUB IN THE WORLD

COME along boys and girls and join the jolliest Club in the world. It is presided over by Bobby Bear and his pals, and that means you will have lots and lots of fun.

Directly you become a member, the postman will bring you a Club Certificate with fine pictures on it which you can hang in your room to show your friends when they call. On meeting another member you can make secret signs, or write in a mysterious secret code. When Club members get together they raise the roof by singing the rollicking Club Song, and we have grand Club Competitions, too.

HOW TO JOIN

If you think all this sounds exciting, and I am sure you do, just fill in your name and address on the label below, cut it out, place both label and token in an unsealed envelope bearing a halfpenny stamp and post to: BOBBY BEAR CLUB, Dept. (X), 68 Long Acre, London, W.C.2.

Bobby Bear will then send you your Club Certificate and also tell you how to obtain the famous enamelled Club Badge, the pride of all members. Come along boys and girls and receive a great big welcome into the Club,
from BOBBY BEAR and AUNT KITEZ.

---- CUT ALONG HERE ----

From
"THE DAILY HERALD" BOBBY BEAR CLUB,
68 LONG ACRE, LONDON, W.C.2.

NAME _____

ADDRESS _____

½d. stamp
MUST BE
affixed to this
space to cover
return postage

Please write clearly in BLOCK CAPITALS

JOIN · THE · BOBBY · BEAR · CLUB · WITHOUT · DELAY ·

---

my peroration: Yesterday author and children's comics expert Denis Gifford stuck up for Biffo and said: 'I think he is suffering because he is an animal. Publishers seem to have decided that readers want to identify with the hero. That means boys and girls reading about boys and girls. I think they are out of touch with their readers. The comics will get very boring.' In other words, as I pointed out in radio interviews there just aren't enough bears reading comics these days.

The nationwide interest shown by modern media in the suspension of a strip cartoon character from a kid's comic will be dismissed by many as typically trivial. The rest of us know better: the life of a cartoon character is more than just ink on paper. Biffo the Bear and his chums become part of the million memories belonging to generations of children. Favourite funny-folk live within us long after we grow out of our comic weeklies, and become as precious to us as our cuddlier companions of the cot. Which brings us to the subject of Teddy Bears.

Biffo the Bear was (hark at me! I mean, *is*—) not a Teddy in the true sense of the term. He bears not the tell-tale dots at the shoulders and hips that mark the *genus teddius bearus* of the comic strip kind. But after all, Teddy-type bears began with real bears—and so, of course, did the strip kind. The first cartoon bears made their debut in an American newspaper, the *San Francisco Examiner*, on June 2nd, 1895. A panel-ful of black and white bear cubs bustled about their business, drawn by Jimmy Swinnerton, destined to become the daddy of the American Sunday Funnies. Jimmy's 'Little Bears' went into colour in 1897, then took the trip to New York with him when Swinnerton was hired by press magnate William Randolph Hearst.

The 'Little Bears' predate the birth of the Teddy Bears, of course, as does the first British bear in comics, Billy Bruin. Billy was one of the mixed menagerie who made up 'Mrs Hippo's Kindergarten', the first strip ever to be published in the *Daily Mirror*. Unfortunately for Billy, April 16th 1904 is better remembered as the birthday of his cartoon classmate, the character who was to emerge from Julius Stafford Baker's crowded panels as the star of the strip—Tiger Tim! After their newspaper debut, Billy, Tim and the rest of the jungle gang moved from the *Mirror* to star in colour in *The Playbox*, the comic supplement to a monthly magazine called *The World and his Wife*. In 1914 they transferred to the front page of a new comic, christened *Rainbow* in honour of its bright colours, where much to their myriad admirers' amazement, Mrs Hippo was transmogrified into Mrs Bruin: a great day for bear lovers everywhere. With the assorted animals rechristened 'The Bruin Boys', Tiger Tim and Co took on a new lease of life, and function to this day within the weekly pages of a comic called *Jack and Jill*. As Tim and his pals often remark, 'Hurrah for Mrs Bruin!'

The first true Teddy Bear strip appeared as a page in the American weekly magazine, *Judge*. The year was 1907 and the cartoonist John Randolph Bray. 'Little Johnny and the Teddy Bears' starred a small boy and his even smaller pets, six little Teds who sported a variety of hats, bow-ties, and pullovers. Their popularity was such

---

(TOP, LEFT) *A mischievous little bear, 'Teddy', who delighted the readers of* The Family Journal. *(CENTRE) Cut-out figures of two perennial favourites, 'Billy Bruin' and 'Mother Bruin'. (LEFT) Application form and details of the popular 'Bobby Bear Club' which boasted over four hundred thousand members!*

First of the full-colour teddies, 'Pipinjay', who with his friends 'Pongo', also a teddy bear, and 'Wogga', the golliwog, ran for years in Fairyland Tales.

that the Thomas A. Edison Company was inspired to produce a trick film called *The Teddy Bears*, in which a number of toy teddies were put through their animated paces in a primitive stop-frame system. This film in turn inspired J. R. Bray to try animating his own cartoon characters, and that led to a completely new career as America's first successful animated cartoon producer.

(TOP) *Japhet and his amusing little bear friend, 'Happy', who appeared in* The Daily News.
(ABOVE) *A true Teddy Bear complete with shoulder and thigh fixings, 'Timothy Tar' drawn by A. E. Breary for* The Star.
(FACING PAGE) *The very first Teddy Bear strip, 'Little Johnny and the Teddy Bears' drawn by John Randolph Bray for the American magazine,* Judge.

Meanwhile, this side of the sea at 25 Bouverie Street, London, the editor of *The Butterfly* was equally inspired. This weekly comic on green paper was already running a strip called 'Little Willie Winks and his Toy City', by Joe Hardman. Little Willie had a collection of magical toys which got up to all manner of mischief. There was a golliwog, a soldier, a couple of wooden dolls—and two Teddy Bears, one black and one white. But such was the contemporary craze for these loveable toys that when he saw Bray's strip in *Judge*, our jovial editor promptly commissioned one of his cartoonists to crib it! Consequently, 'Bobby and the Woolly Bears' burst happily onto the centre spread of *Butterfly* on August 22nd 1908, quite unconcerned about Willy Winks and his Bears on the opposite page, and definitely unconcerned about Little Johnny and his Teddies in *Judge*! To complete the British boom in bears, 'Teddy the Terror of Jungleville School' arrived in *The Family Journal* 'Playground' feature on May 8th 1909. 'The naughtiest scholar in the school' promptly upset the teacher, Miss Giraffe, by upsetting the blackboard on her nose! 'Oh dear! Miss Giraffe was angry! "Teddy, you are expelled!" she cried; while Hippo, the head boy, showed Teddy the quickest way home. But he's sure to be here again next week, Chicks!'

And he was! Ten years later Teddy the Terror was still at it, but better drawn. Herbert Foxwell, who had taken over J. S. Baker's 'Bruin Boys', took over Teddy, too. This was 1919, the year peace came to the people and the comics bloomed again. 'The Teddies', drawn by the prominent children's artist Harry B. Neilson, brought much-needed fun to the pages of the curiously titled comic, *The Sunday Fairy*. A title change to *The Children's Fairy* failed to help, and that was the end of Neilson's Teddies. Another new comic, and much more successful, was *Playtime*, with its assortment of nursery-style characters including 'Bobby Bear'. But apparently the Editor of the new left-wing newspaper *The Daily Herald* was not numbered among the readers of *Playtime*. For in his own Number One, published on March 31st 1919, just two days after No. 1 of *Playtime*, under the title 'Picture Books for the Bairns', who should appear in a cartoon but 'Bobby Bear'!

> *Here's a tale of Bobby Bear,*
> *(See he's standing by the door);*
> *As he meets his mother's stare,*
> *Well he knows what is in store.*
> *For breakfast time is sharp at eight,*
> *And Bobby Bear is* always *late!*

Aunt Kitsie (a Miss Bridges) added a P.S. to the first of her 'Little Talks' to young *Daily Herald* readers. 'I want all of you Kiddies to write to me and tell me what you think of our little Bear, and how you like painting the picture.' Well, all the Kiddies liked him very much, and by the end of 1920 the first collection of Bobby Bear cartoons was on sale for sixpence. Two years later it became *The Bobby Bear Annual*, under which title it came out every Christmas well into the 1950s, long after the daily strip had ceased to be. Bobby Bear wrote his own introduction to his first Annual: 'I must say it is a very grate privilidge for me to have a rele book ritten about miself, but I have alwaze been avery forchnit little bear, tho I have my trubbles to, as you will see in this book. I hope all who rede my advenchurs will injoy them as mutch as I did miself.'

They certainly did, and when the inevitable happened and a Bobby Bear Club was formed, by 1932 the

LITTLE JOHNNY AND THE TEDDY BEARS.

THE TEDS ARE REINDEERS AND JOHN IS SANTA CLAUS; BUT THE TEDS ARE GREEDY, AND A TRAMP COMES ALONG AND AN ACCIDENT HAPPENS.

1. How happy Teddies are because
   John's going to be a Santa Claus,
   While they are hitched up to the sleigh
   To be his reindeers on the way.

2. The silver moon shines on the snow,
   John cracks his whip and off they go.
   Teds know they make a stunning sight.
   No happier Santa rides to night.

3. Now Santa opens up his pack
   And tells the Teds he'll soon be back.
   They trace some candy by the smell,
   And dive into the pack, pell-mell.

4. Just then a hungry tramp comes by
   And Santa's big pack takes his eye.
   He grabs it and starts on a run,
   The Teddies inside, every one.

5. The Teddies growl and scare the tramp
   Just as the big cop nabs the scamp.
   The cop sees bears fly left and right
   And thinks he's lost his senses quite.

6. John loads the Teddies in the sleigh
   While cop walks Mr. Tramp away.
   Then starts for home, and you can bet
   They'll have a happy Christmas yet.

membership clocked a total of four hundred thousand children! Bobby Bear rose to even greater heights of popularity when the panel-and-caption format was changed to a proper daily strip, first drawn by Wilfred Haughton (who also drew the *Mickey Mouse Annuals*), and later by the more stylish Rick Elmes. Somewhat eclipsed today by the continuing success of the *Daily Express* bear 'Rupert' (see elsewhere in this book), Bobby deserves a place in history as the first bear in British newspapers.

But for my own money, or honey, the favourite of all the newspaper bears has to be 'Happy', the cute little cub who so stole the scene in a strip called 'The Adventures of the Noah Family' in *The Daily News* that cartoonist J. F. Horrabin just had to change the title to 'Japhet and Happy'. Boy and bear co-starred cosily from 1924 all the way to the Fifties. Before we leave the newspaper world altogether, a quick flip to 1935 and a swift glance at the short-lived 'Timothy Tar of *The Star*', who appeared in that paper's 'Peter Pan's Corner'. A serial strip by an artist called Breary, Timothy was reborn in the Fifties as 'Teddy Tar', star of several pocket-priced booklets put out by comic publisher L. Miller.

Meanwhile, back in the comics, Teddies toddled amiably along. Arthur White, veteran from the Nineties who would still be at it in the Fifties, drew 'Teddy Tales' in *Chicks' Own* in 1920. Perhaps it would be more correct to say he drew 'Ted-dy Tales', for *Chicks' Own* was that educational oddity, a hyphenated comic. Walter Bell, on his way to becoming a veteran (still at it in the Seventies), began 'Bobbie and his Teddy Bears'

(FACING PAGE) *The very first appearance of the famous British comic strip character, 'Biffo the Bear' drawn by Dudley Watkins for* The Beano.
(ABOVE) *Leo Baxendale's heading for his popular* Beano *strip 'The Three Bears'.*
(BELOW) *'Dennis the Menace' persecutor of Teddy Bear owners— another* Beano *strip from June 30, 1979.* ★

for *The Sunbeam* in 1928. And Herbert Foxwell, not content with his previously mentioned entries, added 'Goldylocks and the Three Bears' to his output in 1920; they appeared in *Tiger Tim's Weekly*. Foxwell was the artist who linked comics and newspapers when he created the weekly 'Teddy Tail' comic supplement for *The Daily Mail*. As there was no bear in the Mrs Whisker mouse household, Foxwell promptly produced 'Cubby and Lulu', a comical couple of cubs, for the 'Jolly Jack' companion comic given free with *The Sunday Dispatch*. As if to even things up, Harry Folkard, son of the originator of 'Teddy Tail', drew a bear strip called 'Paddy Polar' in the *Teddy Tail* comic, and the *Daily Express* promptly put a 'Rupert Bear' strip in their own comic supplement. All this in 1933.

The Thirties was the Golden Age for British comics; indeed, all forms of juvenile publishing flourished. One of the nicest, and today rarest, was a pocket-sized publication put out by John Leng of Dundee. This was *Fairyland Tales*, a weekly mixture of strips and stories aimed at the 'read-to-me-mummy' group. Among the regular favourites was 'Popinjay', a toy teddy who lived in Anthony and Rosemary's nursery along with his chum Wogga the Golly, Jiminy the Spaniel, and an occasional teddy-friend called Pongo. Popinjay had but to hear the call of his friend Adolphus, the teddy bear from down the road, and he was down the drain-pipe in a trice and off on more merry adventures. The illustrator of these anonymous tales was Sam Fair, who turned strip cartoonist in 1938 for Thomson's new comic, *The Dandy*. His character? 'Teddy Bear—The Grizzly Growler on the Prowl!' Popinjay attained some kind of collector's immortality in 1936 when he starred in *Popinjay's Jig-Puz Book*, a unique volume of five full-colour jig-saw puzzles, all for half-a-crown! The Thirties wound up in fine style with 'Sonny Bear and Mickey' arriving on the front page of *The Playbox*,

delightfully drawn by Freddie Crompton; 'Bruno, Lionel and Percy Piggins' drawn by Fred Robinson for *The Golden*; and 'The Three Bears' in *Chicks' Own*, cartooned by Julius Stafford Baker's son, also named Julius.

The Forties were the Dark Ages for comics, with wartime paper shortages limiting size and circulation. Among the odder editions of the time there was *Cubby and the Christmas Star*, a 'Comic and Tracing Book' drawn by now famous comedian Bob Monkhouse, and a one-shot with the unlikely title of *Dizzling Comic*, which reprinted a Dutch strip called 'Terry and Berry the Bears' with a curious and pointless exhortation to 'cut them out, pin them to the wall, and have fun with them!' The decade ended brightly for bears, however, with the brilliant debut of good old Biffo in *The Beano*.

The Fifties saw a small boom in bears. *The Dandy*, not to be outdone by its comical companion, introduced 'Barney's Bear' in 1950. *The Beano* bounced back with 'Little Plum—Your Redskin Chum', a strip by the very individual cartoonist Leo Baxendale. Plum's battles with some hungry bears became a recurring plot which so delighted both editor and readers that by the end of the decade they had spun off into their own strip, 'The Three Bears'. Hugh McNeill, best remembered for his 'Our Ernie' and 'Harold Hare', contributed to the canon by creating 'Teddy and Cuddly' for *Jack and Jill* in 1954.

The Fifties were also the first boom years for Children's Television, and the comics naturally began to reflect that boom. 'Andy Pandy' went onto the front page of the new comic *Robin* (1953), an attempt at producing a nursery school *Eagle*. Naturally the strip featured Andy's partner-in-prankishness, Teddy Bear. 'Sooty', the still-popular hand-puppet manipulated by ventriloquist Harry Corbett, made his first strip appearance in *T.V. Comic* (1954). The artist was Tony Hart, now a tele-personality in his own right, in his own series. When Sooty moved across to *Pippin* in 1967, the art chores were taken on by Fred Robinson, who continues to handle the strip beautifully in the combination comic *Pippin in Playland*. The year 1955 brought the first strip cartoon adaptation of A. A. Milne's 'Winnie the Pooh'. This was in the Ernest Shephard image, not Walt Disney's, and was delightfully drawn for *Playhour* by Peter Woolcock, the artist who had taken over 'The Bruin Boys'.

Television continued to dominate the Sixties, and Hanna-Barbera's 'Yogi Bear' opened the decade with a

weekly appearance in *T.V. Land*. The artist, Chick Henderson, was English. This telly-cartoon character proved so popular that he won his own comic, *Yogi Bear's Own Weekly* (1962), which removed him from another paper he was appearing in at the time, *T.V. Express*. Yogi's comic was no wild success, and was merged into *Huckleberry Hound Weekly* in 1965. Yogi Bear pressed hungrily on, however, and turned up in 1972 in a high-priced paper called *Yogi and His Toy*. The price was high to cover the cost of a Grand Free Gift—every single week! Also from television came 'Tingha and Tucker', a couple of Koalas, who turned up in a comic called *Candy* in 1969. More teddified was 'Bearsworld', a strip in the same comic drawn by John Donnelly. Rolf Harris was another TV star to get himself involved with bears, and in 1966 both Rolf and 'Coojiebear' appeared in *T.V. Toyland*. That real life favourite from the Zoo, 'Pipaluk' the baby polar, popped into *Playland* in 1968. But there was a bit more punch in a character who turned up in 1965's *Storytime* . . . Superbear!

But undoubtedly the historic highspot of the Sixties, or indeed of the whole happy history of comics, as far as Teddy Bear fans are concerned, occurred on September 21st 1963. For on this day was published Number One of a comic wholly devoted to the doings of Teddy Bears and called, with utter appropriateness, *Teddy Bear*! Teddy himself edited the colourful comic from Bear

(ABOVE) 'Dusty Bear' who had his own, short-lived, comic, and (FACING PAGE) 'Teddy Bear' the first Teddy Bear to have a magazine all to himself. 'Winnie the Pooh' now also has his own magazine produced in America by Western Publishing Company and based on the Walt Disney version of the story.

40 PAGES OF FUN FOR LITTLE CHILDREN

Teddy Bear's

SUMMER SPECIAL

35p

Australia 75c,
New Zealand 75c,
Malaysia $3.00

FIND FIVE ICE CREAMS HIDDEN IN PICTURE

Green, Farringdon Street, London, a site unbelievers may claim as the address of Fleetway House. Grand Free Gifts came with the first three issues, including 'My Magic Drawing Book', and as well as appearing on the cover of his comic, Teddy Bear starred in a two-page picture strip with the entire Bear family: Daddy Bear, Mummy Bear, Grandma Bear, Grizzly Bear, Snowy Bear, Bookworm Bear, Fred Bear (a tramp: get it?), Hill Billy Bear, Ivan Bear, and the baby of the family . . . Bare Bear! Among the fun, Teddy found time to deliver such honeyed homilies as 'Never interrupt Mummy when she is talking!' *Teddy Bear* ran for ten years, and still turns up annually in Summer Specials. Even this long life was beaten by 'The Teddy Bears', a strip which began in D. C. Thomson's *Bimbo* in 1961, transferred to *Little Star* in 1972, and bumbles merrily on.

The Seventies saw a decline in comic circulation as the television audience grew, but once again bears bridged the gap. 'Barnaby', created in foreign parts by one Olga Pouchine, was sufficient a hit on British TV to find a place as a strip in *Pippin*, where he is drawn by Jenny Reyn. 'Rupert', transferring to TV from the printed newspaper page, came into comics proper for the first time when *Pippin* started a run of reprints of the Alfred Bestall period, with the added plus of full colour. And 'Teddy Edward', another telly-puppet, turned up in the short-lived *See-Saw* in the form of a photo-strip fumetti. Comics began to close almost as soon as they were launched, taking their teddies with them. New English Library brought out *Dusty Bear Monthly* in 1975, but even a Grand Free Dusty Bear Spaceman Badge failed to get it off the ground. *Toby*, dedicated to a dog but featuring 'Teddy in Toyland', was the first flop of 1976, closely followed by *Magic*. This should have succeeded superbly: well drawn, well coloured it carried the adventures of 'Cuddly and Dudley', who were the naughty nephews, no less, of Biffo the Bear! But *Magic* folded, and the nephews disappeared, perhaps to make a place for their Uncle in the Great Comic in the Sky!

Heaven must be full of bears by now!

'Teddy Bear' the star of the comic which carries his name keeps up with all the latest crazes—like skateboarding in this illustration from a 1979 issue.

THE TIE THAT BINDS.

Birthday Wishes

I 'spect you will get lots of Presents
An' cards an' things ever so fine
But I guess you won't get any Wishes
That 's any more lovin' than mine !

A merry Christmas to you.

GOT A "CIGAWETTE" PICTURE?

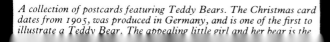

PAUL TERRY'S

TERRY BEARS

THE ANIMATED BEAR

EVER since the earliest days of the animated cartoon, the bear has proved a popular character with animators and public alike. In the very first cartoons the bear was usually the villain of the peace who was outwitted by the hero, but with the passage of time, he became more refined and lovable.

According to Graham Webb, an expert on the animated cartoon who provided much of the material for this section, the earliest bear character was Cubby Bear, a black cub who was created by Van Buren in the early 1930s. True to most of this artist's creations he was devoid of any real character and was little more than a figure to put into gag situations.

That oldest of bear stories, Goldilocks and the Three Bears, early attracted the attentions of the animators, and in 1924 Walt Disney himself parodied the tale in 'Alice and the Three Bears'. The bears need a grasshopper to provide 'hops' in their stew, but failing to find one settle for Alice—actually a live-action girl in a cartoon world. The anarchist cartoon maker, Tex Avery, also delighted in slaughtering fairy tales and in his 'The Bear's Tale' (1940) he mixed Goldilocks and the Three Bears with Little Red Riding Hood and the wolf to produce absolutely chaotic results.

Perhaps the first major bear character to be launched was Barney Bear who appeared in 1939 in a short called 'The Bear That Couldn't Sleep' made by Rudolf Ising. His initial concept was as a slow thinking and acting bear, and in this first picture Barney spends the whole of his hibernation period trying to stop all the noise going on around him. A year later, when Barney returned to the screen again, he was still slow-moving and lazy, but had become a well-meaning blunderer. By the end of his 30-film career he was a much loved busybody who usually got the worst of whatever happened to be heading his way.

The industrious Tex Avery came up with two more bear characters in the mid-forties who are still remembered today. They were George and Junior, two hobo bears modelled on John Steinbeck's characters in his famous novel, 'Of Mice and Men'. George, the so-called brains of the partnership, was always thinking of new money-making (or food-getting) schemes for Junior to foul-up!

Walt Disney had become well aware of the appeal of bears on the screen, and came up with one of the most memorable in the splendidly slow-witted, but violent-when-aroused Br'er Bear in 'Song of the South', a feature length film made in 1946. Br'er Bear was a brilliant foil for the sly and cunning Br'er Fox and was forever claiming he was going to 'Knock his head clean off' when he realised he had been cheated yet again.

A year later Disney transformed a story by another famous American author, Sinclair Lewis, entitled 'Bongo' to the screen as a part of the cartoon feature, 'Fun and Fancy Free'. This story is just full of bears. It recounts how Bongo, a unicycle-riding bear tires of circus life and goes to find his relatives in the forest. There he meets and falls in !ove with Lulubelle, and has to fight for her affections with another bear named Lumpjaw. The highlight of this delightful film is surely the dancing sequence where the bears sing and dance in square-dance fashion to a tune 'Say It With A Slap' in

(FACING PAGE) *The lively and popular 'Terry Bears' and Walt Disney's engaging 'Bongo' and 'Lulubelle' from the film 'Fun and Fancy Free'.*
(ABOVE) *The loveable 'Andy Panda' and Tex Avery's scheming partnership, 'George and Junior'.*

which they underline the old adage that when a bear is in love he says it with a slap. . . .

Utilising once again the Three Bears idea, Chuck Jones at Warner Brothers next gave the world his Three Bears series. Making their first appearance in a 1944 cartoon 'Bugs Bunny and the Three Bears', the trio went on a few years later to star in their own pictures. The quick tempered Papa Bear usually made his oversized son, Junior, carry out all his dirty work while Mama Bear, wanting nothing more than a peaceful life, would just look on and say 'Yes, Dear!' at appropriate intervals.

Strangely, after such an initial burst of enthusiasm for bears in animated films, there was a hiatus of nearly five years before the next ones appeared in cartoons. In the early 1950s, Terrytoons suddenly decided to make a series under the uncribbable title of The Terry Bears. Their debut was actually in 1951 in a film called 'Tall Timber Tales' in which the two mischievous cubs caused their Papa bear no end of trouble with their pranks.

It was almost inevitably Walt Disney who gave the bear syndrome a totally new character when he brought the very first Teddy Bear to the screen—in his famous version of 'Peter Pan'. The Teddy Bear belonged to the smallest of the children, Michael, and was carried by him throughout the entire picture—except when he was captured by Indians and the bear was seen tied to a stake of his own! It is an interesting fact that Teddy Bears had only just been created when Sir J. M. Barrie wrote the original story in 1904.

In the more traditional style, Disney gave us a sequence in the film 'Hold That Pose' in which Goofy tried to photograph a bear. What happened was that a new character was born in Humphrey, a greedy National Park bear who was always having run-ins with the Park Ranger. Seems familiar? Well, Jack Hannah, who conceived the idea, shortly afterwards left the Disney studios and went to work for Walter Lantz where he created a similar series about a bear called 'Fatso'. Unfortunately the series failed—but the idea lived on in Hanna-Barbera's 'Yogi Bear' which is still popular today.

Hanna-Barbera have, of course, gone on to put many other bears into their made-for-television series: The Hillbilly Bears, Breezly & Sneezly (a Polar Bear and a seal), Blubber Bear (who appeared in 'Whacky Races), the Hair Bear Bunch (a gang of bears in a zoo) and the C. B. Bears. But of all these, Yogi and his little side-kick, Boo Boo, still remain the most successful. Yogi got his name from a famous American baseball player called

'The Three Bears' created by Chuck Jones—the docile Mama and Junior and highly volatile Papa Bear.

'Yogi' Berra and his voice was based on that of a TV actor named Art Carney being imitated by the multi-voiced Daws Butler. It is perhaps not well known that Yogi also had a girl friend, Cindy who appeared occasionally in the TV shows and the feature film, 'Hey There! It's Yogi Bear'.

Among other more recent cartoon bears that should be mentioned are the father and son act, Windy and Breezy, made by Walter Lantz: 'The Beary Family' rather like an up-dated version of Chuck Jones' Three

(TOP) *One of the few true Teddy Bear stars of the screen, Michael's Teddy, who appeared in the Walt Disney version of the famous story, 'Peter Pan'.*
(BOTTOM) *Two of the best loved bears in animated films—'Barney Bear' and 'Br'er Bear' who appeared in Disney's 'Song of the South'.*

(ABOVE) *The memorable 'Baloo' from Disney's 'Jungle Book'.*
(RIGHT) *The irrepressible 'Yogi Bear' and* (BELOW) *'The Hair Bear Bunch'—'Square Bear', 'Hair Bear' and 'Bubi Bear'—both cartoon series produced by Hanna-Barbera.*

Bears; and Terrytoons rather lack-lustre character in 'Possible Possum'.

Perhaps not surprisingly, Disney was opened our saga of bears on the screen, also closes it. In 1966 he made a twenty-six minute short film, 'Winnie the Pooh and the Honey Tree' which, though popular in America, infuriated many English fans of the story because a new character, a gopher, was introduced at the expense of Piglet. Nonetheless, the picture was successful enough for two sequels to be made 'Winnie the Pooh and the Blustery Day' (1969) which won an Academy Award and 'Winnie the Pooh and Tigger too' (1975). Later all three were amalgamated to make a main feature which, though the style may have been somewhat removed from the vision of A. A. Milne and Ernest Shepard, did help bring the lovable little bear and his friends to a whole new generation of admirers.

Equally, many enthusiasts of Rudyard Kipling's classic *Jungle Book* may have found things to quarrel with in Disney's recent version of this wonderful story. But there can be no denying they made Baloo the Bear a memorable and very lovable character.

SOME HUGS[*] OF TEDDY BEARS

* HUG—a collection or gathering of Teddy Bears

TO most Teddy Bear owners, their little friends are beyond price and—if you'll excuse the pun—they could not bear to part with them. But in recent years a demand has grown up among collectors all over the world, in particular America, for veteran and vintage bears which has resulted in them fetching high prices when they do change hands. Although these prices are subject to continuous change, it is possible to give a few guidelines.

Naturally enough it is impossible to put a value on the very first Teddy Bears made by Morris Michtom in America and Margarete Steiff in Germany, and the few surviving examples are now museum pieces. One of Michtom's bears, for example, being on display in the Smithsonian Museum in Washington, and an early Steiff enjoying a place of honour in the town of Giengen.

After these precious rarities, the most sought after Teddies are the early models, now in their seventies, which were stuffed with straw and had humps on their backs. A well-preserved example complete with long snout, boot-button eyes, long arms and big feet would fetch more than £50 in Britain and perhaps as much as $200 in the United States.

One of the long-nosed bears made without a hump in the early 1920s would almost certainly fetch around £30, but strangely is not as valuable in the eyes of collectors as the large, snub-nosed bears made in the 1950s. Apparently one of these 'with character' can command as much as £45. Even youthful Teddies from the late fifties and sixties now have their devoted admirers prepared to pay quite handsomely to add new examples to their collections.

Perhaps the best instance that can be cited of this

(ABOVE) *Matt Murphy of America, owner of the largest collection of Teddy Bears in the world.*
(BELOW) *Some of the players in Matt Murphy's football team, who have practices, authentic matches and even league tables!*

A bevy of beauties—ladies and Teddy Bears! (ABOVE) *Austrian arctophile, Dr. Traude Motzko* (BELOW, RIGHT) *an unknown admirer with six-foot 'Teddy' and 'Panda', and* (LEFT) *Colyn Saal of Queensland, Australia, with another six-foot bear, handmade by her family, and named 'Fred Humphrey Tuttle'.*

booming market occurred in 1974 when a much pummelled Winnie-the-Pooh was sold by Jill Abrahams of Manhattan for $150, about £60!

It is in America that the largest collections of Teddy Bears are to be found—and the biggest hug in the world is undoubtedly that of Matt Murphy of Dallas, Texas who, at the time of writing, has well over *eleven hundred* bears of all sorts and sizes, drawn from over 135 countries! Matt, a banker by profession, has a special den in his home for this enormous assembly which includes bears made in everything from chocolate, leather, whalebone to walrus tusk and even gold.

Matt first became fascinated with bears at six years old when his parents brought him a dozen German miniature bears to help him recover from an operation to remove his tonsils.

'I took those first Teddy Bears and played with them the way kids do with toy soldiers', he says. 'My mother dressed them up for me. I added to the collection until I had 36. We were living in California then and I was a fan of the University of California Football Team. I dressed up the whole team of bears like the Golden Bears football players and instead of names, I gave them numbers.'

Matt also invented a game with the bears where the plays were determined by a throw of a dice. He still continues the games today, and runs a whole season of matches keeping a list of results and a league table.*

* Our own eldest son, Richard, now 13, also devised numerous games with his group of 'Teds', compiling league tables based on their results. We suspect many other small children have done—and do—the same sort of thing.

Perhaps the most unusual item in his collection is a collage of a Teddy Bear inside a tennis racquet—a combination of the two great interests in his life. For apart from his collection of bears, Matt is a keen tennis fan and it is a fact that while he was a young man living in Ireland he played for a time in the Irish Davis Cup Team.

Another San Franciscan, Victor Davis, a real estate millionaire, is a similarly dedicated collector and has examples from all over the world in his assembly of 800.

Although these two gentlemen possess by far the largest collections in America, there are two ladies equally determined and energetic in their collecting. The lady with the biggest assembly is Virginia Walker who houses her group of over 600 bears in a residence in Manatee County which she most appropriately calls 'Teddy Towers'. Mary Ann Rhoads who lives in Los Angeles has the next largest collection of over 300 bears.

The largest collection consisting entirely of Teddy Bears belongs to James Walt of Flushing in Michigan, who, not surprisingly, is known among the fraternity of archtophilists as 'The Teddy Baron'. He has been collecting since he was 14 years old and at the last count had in excess of 250 Teddies overflowing the shelves and rooms of his home. The star members of his hug are 'Ambidexterous Jones' and 'Sir Tubbs de Squaretoes'.

Perhaps the most unusual collection of Teddy Bears in America is that belonging to Mrs. Patricia Fitt of Hamden, Connecticut. She has created the 'Bear House Workshop'—44 different rooms made from boxes in which live 74 Teddies not one over four inches tall. The rooms are filled with tiny pieces of furniture and virtually make up a town with a kitchen, pantry, theatre

(FACING PAGE) *James Walt of Michigan 'The Teddy Baron' with some of the collection he has been amassing since he was 14.*
(ABOVE) *The star member of Andrea Way's collection in Boston, and her original letter-heading motif.*
(BELOW, RIGHT) *Miss Sheila Coull of Edinburgh with some of her 'hug'.*

(complete with scenery and props for a production of 'Macbeth'), nursery, library, music room, school room, laundry, pool room, work shop, two bathrooms, two dinings rooms, a general store, butchers, post office, hostel, stable, playground, marina, chapel and even a Buddhist temple! Among the most distinguished residents are 'Fat Face' (at 15, the oldest), 'Lion Bear' who has a toupee which is actually a mane, 'Simon Barsinister' the stubborn butcher, 'Ivan the Terribear' (from Russia, naturally) and 'Mousey Tongue Bear' a revolutionary who belongs to the leftist United Brown Bear Brothers, a movement led by one 'H. Rap Bear'!

In Great Britain, the largest collection of bears is without doubt that of retired Army Colonel Bob Henderson of Edinburgh who, at the time this book was being written, had 462 of all kinds measuring from 0.3 inches to three feet tall. No doubt the number has increased since then!

The Colonel's collection is quite unique and beside over one hundred of the popular type of cuddly Teddy Bears, he has model bears in the shape of moneyboxes, tea-pots, cruet sets, candles, paper-weights, chessmen, bottles, cake ornaments, table ornaments, matchboxes, tobacco jars, brooches, souvenirs, pendants, castings, carvings, fretwork, shoes, umbrella stands, puppets and ash trays. They are made of plastic, wax, soap, papier-mache, cardboard, wood, china, earthenware, glass, fur, paper, sugar, marzipan, chocolate, stone, soapstone, bone, ivory, gold, silver, bronze, brass, lead, pipe cleaners, etc.

Colonel Bob, as he is affectionately known, is especially proud of his 1903 Teddy Bear, a 'Mark I' model as he calls it. This bear, a year older than the Colonel, started life as the property of his elder brother, and then was shared by the two boys. It was inherited by the Colonel's daughter, Cynthia, and promptly changed sex! The little girl dressed it in a frilly skirt and the bear who had previously been 'Teddy Boy' became 'Teddy Girl'. She is today possibly the oldest—and certainly the best preserved—Teddy in the U.K.

(ABOVE) *A model of Winnie the Pooh made in flannel which is now much sought-after by collectors of bears.*

(FACING PAGE) *Colonel Bob Henderson with some of his remarkable collection of bears. He is holding 'Teddy Girl' who has been in his family for over seventy years and was considered a male Teddy Bear until the Colonel's daughter insisted on dressing 'him' in a skirt and re-naming the bear 'Teddy Girl'. The article below on 'Collecting Bears' was written by Colonel Henderson.*

The next oldest bear in the Colonel's collection is 'Tibby'. Bought in Selfridge's in London in 1909, he travelled all over the world with his owner and her father, a film director of documentaries about native life and animals. In Africa, 'Tibby' was regarded with awe by the native tribesmen and treated as a 'familiar' or 'spirit'. Later he went to Mauritius, Australia and home to America via the South Sea Islands. On the death of his owner in 1968, he returned to the U.K., thereby ending his tour completely round the world in just under 60 years! Another distinguished member of the collection is 'Growly' whose growl was recorded by the B.B.C. for their sound archives!

The Colonel did not set out deliberately to make a collection of bears, he explains. It would be more accurate to say that he has an accumulation of bears. There are Teddies left over from his childhood, others his daughter acquired when she was young, and more were added for his granddaughter to play with. Many of the bear models were presents from friends who found them on travels abroad. Others were sent to him by people living in various countries. Quite a number are souvenirs from places he has visited. The Colonel also has a prize-winning collection of postage stamps devoted entirely to stamps which feature bears.

Colonel Bob says the whole thing arose out of his investigation into the phenomena of 'Teddy Bear Consciousness' that he found to be so widespread in the adult world. Whilst engaged in this pursuit, he has brought together many Teddy Bear lovers and helped them to form their own groups, and as a result of this they dubbed him 'President of the Teddy Bear Club' in 1962. Then, in 1970, with American journalist, Jim Ownby, he was a founder member of the 'Good Bears of the World' movement which is discussed in detail later in this book.

Edinburgh also boasts another large collection of 215

COLLECTING BEARS

THE HOBBY OF COLLECTING models of bears is called Arctophily. Lovers of bears are arctophiles and collectors of bear-like models - arctophilists. These words are derived from the Greek words "arktos" bear, and "philos" friend or lover, in the same way as Arctic and Arcadia (Bear Country) and the name Arthur (Bear Man).

Every model bear in a collection tells a story, and by association has links with people, places or things: especially a Teddy Bear. That is how a collection of bears grows. The bears are souvenirs as well as symbols of love, friendship, happiness and security.

Collecting bears in this way is a most enjoyable pastime. It appeals to the hunting instinct (without cruelty). Wherever you go you can look around for specimans. It is a great game that can be played anywhere, at anytime, and for as long as you like at each occasion. And you will find that every bear tells a different story. Therein lies their widespread interest.

There are no bears in Australia, but the Koala looks like a bear, so much so in fact that it is frequently referred to as a bear - the Australian tree-bear. Likewise in China, the Giant Panda which is the largest member of the raccoon family, is called the white bear. Accordingly, Koalas and Giant Pandas are included in the fold when it comes to collecting model bears.

A model bear, especially a Teddy Bear, and more especially a friendly-looking soft and cuddly one, serves as a totem, that is an outward symbol of an existing intimate unseen relationship. If it is a good model, or a good Teddy-bear, it is a good totem or motif.

From this point of view the word model should be considered in both senses of its two meanings, namely as a three-dimensional imitation, generally in miniature, and also as a pattern of excellence. Only model models

of the bear are worthy of being called "Good Bears of the World".

As the collection grows it attracts the interest of like-minded people, who can then group together to form a local Teddy Bear Club. Quite a number of people in both the USA and UK as well as in the rest of Europe and elsewhere, have formed small dens around collections in this way. The members of the groups have great fun comparing notes and helping each other by sharing bear stories. Or organizing teddy-bear picnics for children. These groups should now be developed into GBW dens, and so spread the good work of the GBW association.

Once a collection becomes known, bears come to one from all directions on all sorts of occasions, just because they are souvenirs of so many different associations. In fact, they appear to multiply like rabbits.

The remarkable 'Bear House Workshop' belonging to Mrs. Patricia Fitt of Connecticut which features some 74 little Steiff Teddy Bears in tableaux of various rooms, shops and buildings. The photographs on the facing page show the work shop and school room, while in the picture above, Mrs. Fitt's daughter, Ann, sits before part of the array of rooms which makes her home such a wonderland for any arctophile!

bears in the home of Miss Sheila Coull, but the lady with the biggest collection in the British Isles is actually Mrs. Audrey Duck who lives in Whitton, Middlesex and has over 240. However, the 'Queen of the Teddy Bears' is actress Jean Barrington from Wolverhampton who has over 150 of them. Whenever she is away from home appearing on the stage she always takes two of the bears, 'Barney' and 'Berney' along with her to ensure her good luck. A photograph on these pages shows Jean with Colonel Bob surely the 'King of Teddy Bears'.

Colonel Henderson as the self-appointed historian of the Teddy Bear, says that he has a nominal roll of over 60 collectors of bears, of which 45 are in the U.K. But with the huge number of bears manufactured and sold

every year, the number of people consciously or unconsciously, determinedly or casually collecting them throughout the world must run into millions.

There are, of course, quite a number of famous people who, over the years, have professed to owning Teddy Bears. Our own Prince Charles, the heir to the Throne, for example, took his favourite Teddy Bear to prep school, and the much-loved American President John F. Kennedy and his successor, Lyndon Johnson, both had Teddies for most of their lives—continuing the tradition begun by their illustrious predecessor, Theodore Roosevelt, of course. The recently disgraced President Nixon, however, was not so lucky and once admitted, 'To the extent of not having a Teddy Bear, my early childhood might be described as disadvantaged'.

British member of Parliament, Clement Freud, still cherishes his childhood Teddy and said recently, 'If you have a Teddy Bear I don't see how you could ever get rid of it. After all there's no scheme for pensioning off old Teddy Bears.'

People from the world of entertainment seem to be particularly fond of Teddy Bears. The singer Elvis Presley who died so tragically had a bear from his childhood, and after recording the famous song 'I Just Want To Be Your Teddy Bear' was deluged with Teddy Bears and bear mascots of all kinds by his delighted fans. One newspaper reported that he received almost two

(ABOVE) *Actress Jean Barrington, known as 'Queen of the Teddy Bears', has a collection of over 150 bears at her home in Wolverhampton. Here she is proudly showing off her 'hug' to the man who might be called 'King of the Teddy Bears', Colonel Bob Henderson.*
(BELOW) *'The Teddy Lady of Portland', Jeannie Miller of Oregon, has over 100 bears, including a unique Teddy called 'Brandy'—which she is holding here—who has a heart-beat powered by an electric battery and has been used to soothe new born babies.*
(FACING PAGE) *Teddies, like children, love Christmas! A delightful photograph of two of the bears from her collection taken by Dinah Cody of Chicago.*

thousand such gifts and if this is true it would make his collection (assuming it is still together) by far the largest in the world!

Peter Bull the actor and raconteur has played a very important part in promoting the cause of the Teddy Bear, and with his particular friend, Theodore, has delighted audiences of all ages on both sides of the Atlantic. Peter's books, *Bear With Me* (1969) and *Peter Bull's Book of Teddy Bears* (1971) are required reading for anyone interested in the subject. Sir John Betjeman, the Poet Laureate, also has a very special bear called 'Archibald Ormsby-Gore' who has been immortalised in his owner's marvellous autobiographical verses, 'Summoned by Bells' and in his own special book, *Archie and the Strict Baptists* (1977).

Among other stars who proudly display their Teddy friends, let us just mention actor Dustin Hoffman, actresses Jill Bennet and Samantha Eggar (who actually carried her Teddy Bear at her wedding), ballerina Margot Fonteyn, and singers Dusty Springfield (who calls hers 'Einstein') and Anita Harris. Anita started

(ABOVE) *'Dunky-Dick' the Teddy Bear mascot of the Scottish team at the British Commonwealth Games in Edinburgh in 1970. The bear was named after Mr. Dunky Wright, a former Scottish marathon gold medallist, and Mr. Dick, the Scottish team coach.*

(FACING PAGE) *Actor Peter Bull who has done so much for the Teddy Bear cause. In the photograph he appears with his little bear, 'Theodore' and singer, Dusty Springfield, and her much-loved companion, 'Einstein'.*

collecting Teddy Bears when she was given one as a present by a fan; this was later followed by others and now they are all numbered 'Teddy Bear 1', 'Teddy Bear 2' and so on.

All these people, the famous and the ordinary collectors, have played a part in the history of the Teddy Bear, and after a brief pause to look at some of the record breaking bears, we shall be considering the development of the 'Good Bears of the World' movement which now brings supporters and collectors together in a global hug of friendship. . . .

The bear facts about Peter Bull

Collectors' World: Friday 8.0 BBC2 Colour

'Much cheaper than a psychiatrist, and not nearly as supercilious,' is one of the many pungent yet affectionate remarks that Peter Bull has, in his time, made on the subject of the Teddy Bear. Mr Bull and his collection of 40 assorted bears, the fruit of a lifelong obsession, are featured this week in the first of a new series called **Collectors' World**.

Just as animal lovers often

It's a traumatic experience- having your teddy bear taken away from you

grow to resemble their (live) pets, or devoted married couples acquire an odd likeness to each other, so Mr Bull looks something like a large, amiable bear himself. He is a familiar face, from films (Dr Strangelove, Tom Jones, Dr Dolittle) ...stage (Waiting for Godot, Luther). He is also a splendid example of a declining breed, the gentleman amateur actor, writer, traveller and wit. When he is not hard at work in England or America, he lives on Paxos, a small Greek island near Corfu. The BBC caught him on a visit to London and discussed his collection with him.

His passion for teddy bears dates from his childhood, and in particular from a dreadful incident when he returned home from school to find that something had happened to his beloved teddy. As the programme shows, he cannot remember the details without pain to this day.

Last year his book about bears, whimsically entitled *Bear With Me*, was published. It is a semi-serious collection of anecdotes and musings on the history and significance of teddies. Apparently Theodore Roosevelt was responsible for starting the craze in America in 1902; but they soon caught on here, and the English have produced some classic bears of fiction, like Winnie the Pooh, and Aloysius in Evelyn Waugh's *Brideshead Revisited*.

'Englishmen are far more ready to confess that they cling to their bears than Americans,'

THE MAKING OF TEDDY

Behind the scenes in a Teddy Bear factory. Perhaps these photographs might be a little unsuitable to show impressionable young Teddies, but this is really how they are created in the factory of Dean's Childsplay Toys in Rye, Sussex. First the material is cut to shape and assembled. Then they are hand-filled or blow-filled with foam according to their size. The sewers then sew up the openings and finishers add the noses, mouths, eyes, etc, to complete the process. The display of bears (BELOW) are typical of the Dean's range, while the appealing little chap on the left is from the range of another manufacturer of Teddies, Merrythought Ltd.

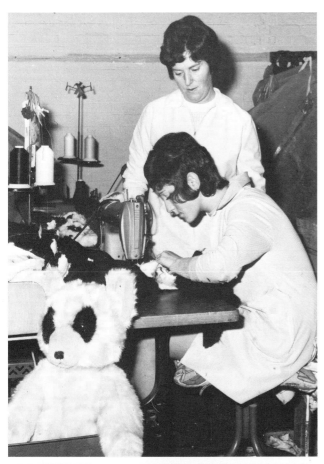

THE TEDDIES' BOOK OF RECORDS

SO DAISY HAS VOWED TO MAKE 400,000 TEDDY BEARS

A YEAR ago Mrs Daisy Clark, Stobhill, Morpeth, spent three months in hospital.

To pass the time, she made Teddy bears from fur fabric. Orders came in from other patients, visitors, and staff.

Some patients she met had cancer. So she decided to put all the money she made into a fund to buy a £250,000 body-scanning machine for Newcastle General Hospital.

When she left hospital, she made more and more bears and sold them for £2.50 each.

Her husband, Charlie, helped by cutting out the pieces and doing the stuffing.

They even took a stall at a local market to sell the bears!

Then, six months ago, Charlie died of a heart attack.

But Daisy went on making her bears. She found it helped her in her grief. Because she couldn't sleep, she got up at four-thirty to sew.

By Christmas she'd raised £5000 —in a single year!

NOW she has so many orders for bears she's recruited friends to help.

One cuts out the pi... to sew. A school... the bear...

RAREST

Although the early Teddy Bears made by Morris Michtom and Margarete Steiff might be thought to be the rarest, the honour in fact belongs to 'Peter the bear' a line of Teddies made between 1925 and 1928 by the Gebrüder Süssenguth factory in Neustadt near Coburg. Peter was a completely unique bear in that he had a very realistic face, glass eyes that rolled from side to side, and a mouth that opened to reveal a moving tongue and two rows of sharp, curved wooden teeth. He was also fitted with a 'growler' which was particularly loud and realistic and to the extent that it is said that whenever they were sent through the post they made such strange noises the parcels were invariably opened to see what was inside! It is a sad fact that these cleverly made but ferocious bears obviously frightened their young owners and put off adults so that few survived more than a few years before being discarded. The illustrations here show the Peter bears were quite unlike any other Teddy Bear ever made.

SMALLEST

Colonel Bon Henderson—'Mr. Teddy' himself—owns what is believed to be the smallest model bear in the world, a tiny silver replica which measures just 0.3 inches from tip to toe. The Colonel has to keep a very close watch on him among all his other hundreds of bears in case he goes missing. The smallest actual Teddy Bear in the same collection is just one inch tall.

'Sir Gangy de Brownman, Bt.' who moves in the highest circles and can claim among his friends Sir Alec Rose's rabbit mascot who sailed around the world with the intrepid yachtsman. *'Sir Gangy'* has one of the largest wardrobes of any Teddy Bear ranging from a full admiral's uniform to this stylish country outfit.

BIGGEST

The biggest Teddy Bear in the world is 'Mr. Happy' who is almost twice the height of a tall man and as wide across the middle as three average men! He is actually too bulky to stand upright, but measures over twelve feet from the crown of his head to the soles of his feet. He was on display at the time of the 1975 Summer Fair in Edinburgh and was rather unkindly nick-named 'Ugly Bear' by some visitors! He has been rather shy about appearing in public ever since.

1903

OLDEST

The record of being the oldest Teddy Bear is an honour that must be jointly shared by one of Margarete Steiff's bears known as 'Friend Petz' which has a place of honour in the Steiff Offices in Giengen, and 'Teddy's Bear' made by Morris Michtom and sent to President Roosevelt in Washington and now on permanent display in the Smithsonian Institute. Both, of course, were created in 1903 and can be regarded as the 'parents' of the millions of Teddy Bears now found all over the world. To some people they are the 'Adam and Eve' of the Teddy Bear World!

FASTEST

The fastest Teddy Bear on earth is certainly 'Mr. Woppit' who belonged to the late Donald Campbell. Mr. Campbell of course broke world speed records on both land and water and he always had his little friend with him in the cockpit on these attempts. 'Mr. Woppit', with his slightly foxy appearance, was actually first created as a character for the children's comic *Robin* in 1953, but when the magazine's deputy editor, Peter Barker, later became Donald Campbell's manager, he gave a model of the bear to the speedman as a good luck mascot. The two were inseparable thereafter. In May 1959 Donald and 'Mr. Woppit' broke the world's water speed record with a speed of 260.3 miles per hour in the jet-propelled Bluebird hydroplane on Coniston Water. The following year, on the Bonneville Salt Flats in Utah, they miraculously survived the fastest car crash in history when Campbell's Proteus Bluebird car hit a patch of wet sand and went out of control. When Mr. Campbell regained consciousness in hospital his first thought was of 'Mr. Woppit'—who was discovered still in the shattered cockpit but suffering nothing worse than a slightly disjointed nose! Later the two companions successfully pushed the land speed record up to 403 m.p.h. Tragically, they were also together when Donald Campbell was killed in a crash on Coniston Water attempting another speed record in January 1967. 'Mr. Woppit', though, was found floating in the water and was passed into the safe keeping of Mr. Campbell's widow. Since then he has lived quietly in retirement.

HIGHEST

Although quite a few Teddy Bears have been with their owners to the tops of very high mountains like the Matterhorn and other peaks in the Alps, the world's highest flying Teddy reached an altitude of 12,000 feet in 1977. He was taking part in the making of a film called 'Falling Angels' about sky diving and appeared in a breath-taking sequence in company with two young girls named Sally and Teresa. They all leapt from an aeroplane with Teddy in the middle and dived for many thousands of feet before finally releasing their parachutes. Although Teddy apparently showed not a moment's unease during his record-breaking dive, he did insist on wearing his own parachute just in case of emergencies!

(RIGHT) *'Zissi the Bear' who climbed the Matterhorn with Walter Bonatti in February 1965, going up the treacherous North Face. A brave partnership of man and Teddy!*

BRAVEST

The accolade of being the bravest Teddy Bear belongs to the explorer-Teddy named 'Major Laing', whose fame now extends from his home in Broadway, Worcestershire to Timbuctu in the Republic of Mali where he showed great courage in 1972. The Teddy is in fact named after Major Gordon Laing, the first white man to reach Timbuctu in 1826, and who was also murdered there. In November 1972, 'Major Laing's' owner, Mrs. Ruth de la Mare, along with her husband, went to Timbuctu and had some hair-raising moments as they traversed the Niger River Valley. Apparently the local native children had never seen a Teddy Bear before and were amazed at their little visitor. Fortunately their amazement did not go to the lengths of treating the bear in the same way as his namesake, and the brave little chap eventually reached home none the worse for his experiences!

BEST SELLING BOOK

The single best selling title featuring a Teddy Bear is undoubtedly *Winnie the Pooh* by A. A. Milne first published in 1926. It has been translated into twenty-two languages (including Latin, Esperanto and Initial Teaching Alphabet), and in America alone over ten million hardback copies have been sold in the fifty-odd years since it first appeared. In Britain the paperback edition sells over 100,000 copies annually, and even the hardcover climbs into the best selling lists from time to time. The book is also a best seller in Russia where over 400,000 copies of the adventures of 'Vinni-Pukh'—as Winnie is called—have been sold in the last ten years. As a matter of public record, Winnie the Pooh was named after a real bear called 'Winnie' at the London Zoo in the early twenties, and Pooh after a swan that the Milne family saw at Angmering in Sussex.

MOST TRAVELLED

'Edward Bear' who belonged to four-year-old Jamie Fowler of Wellington, New Zealand established the record mileage travelled by a Teddy Bear when he logged 150,000 miles and was in the air for over 300 hours of flying in the summer of 1975—and it all happened by mistake! Unfortunately, James, who was on his way from New Zealand for a holiday in London, made a stop-over in Los Angeles on June 21st and there left Edward on his seat. When a kind-hearted stewardess saw the forlorn Teddy, she set him off in search of his owner—a journey by various planes which took him via London, Copenhagen, Johannesburg, Hong Kong, Rio de Janeiro, Tahiti, Jamaica, Bermuda, New York and, finally, to Los Angeles where amazingly he caught up with Jamie on his return flight to New Zealand on September 7th! Even then he nearly got sent off to the Far East, when, covered with labels, he was left for a moment by Jamie and another helpful stewardess was just about to put him on board a DC 10 bound for Singapore!

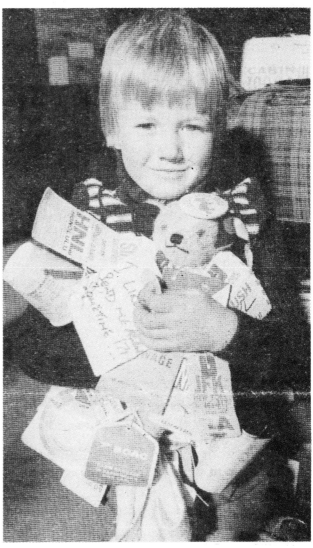

MOST VALUABLE

Currently the most valuable Teddy Bear was the one which appeared with the famous American child star Shirley Temple in her film, 'Captain January' (1936) made by Twentieth Century Fox. A few years back, in 1978, Twentieth Century held a mammoth auction of many of their old studio props and under the hammer went the largish, dark brown bear—fetching a record price of $450 (almost £220) from the lucky purchaser. As a matter of interest the most expensive Teddy Bear that can be bought today is an 18 inch high Teddy made in mink which is sold in the London store of Fortnum & Mason for £125.50 each.

Teddy Bears

In recent years, some sinister Teddy bears have been found with unhealthy insides that might well harm their owners in the latters' more carnivorous moments. So we decided to investigate Teddy bears. We have carried out post-mortems on 40, all except one of them, British subjects. The odd one came from China.

In order to give you a report for Christmas, we had to buy the bears during the summer, so you may find some in the shops that escaped our net – bears that hibernate in the summer and come out for Christmas.

The bears came in all sorts of different colours, shapes and sizes, some traditional, some less so. We set out to assess how safely they were made.

We tried to test the bears in their most popular sizes – from 8½ inches to nearly 3 fe...

Skins
Most bears had a ...
with a p...
...

It is important that their stuffings should be clean, and that they should not contain any harmful substances that a child can suck out.

The Rag Flock and Other Filling Materials Regulations, 1961 and 1965, lay down requirements for the cleanliness of some stuffings, and there are proposals to cover most other types.

Most of the fillings we examined were satisfactory, passing existing or proposed standards. A few failed tests for technical reasons, but there was little wrong with any of the stuffings.

Voices
Some bears had voices (see Table), usually like bleating sheep. Sonia emitted a chime.

The Patkin Anim... Ted...
in its right leg th...

WEALTHIEST

According to recent newspaper reports, Paddington Bear is the wealthiest Bear in the world, for he earns over *£5 million pounds a year* through the use of his name on over 200 products ranging from books, badges, stickers, T-shirts, clothing, wallpaper, furnishing and even chocolate moulds! Paddington also holds another world record according to his creator, Michael Bond—a golfing record. For not so long ago he won a prize for the longest shot by hitting a golf ball with a broken club onto a train which then travelled nine miles before stopping!

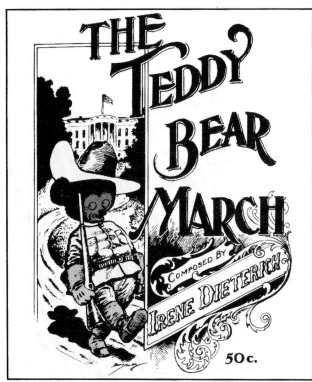

THE TEDDY BEAR MARCH

COMPOSED BY IRENE DIETERICH

50¢.

MOST DANGEROUS

Although Teddy Bears are manufactured in a great many countries, those from Poland have more than once been in trouble because of their contents. The British Home Office issued a warning in 1973 against imported Teddy Bears from Poland which were said to be stuffed with a powdered resin mixed with wood shavings. In this powder was found a toxic chemical called formaldehyde which is particularly dangerous to children when swallowed or inhaled. The Home Office has also warned against certain bears originating from Hong Kong which are believed to give off poisonous fumes when left in front of a fire or pressed against a hot water bottle. In an effort to prevent dangerous Teddy Bears reaching children, *Which*, the Consumers' Association magazine conducted an investigation into a cross section of bears in December 1967.

BEST SELLING SONG

There have been something like fifty songs written about the Teddy Bear in the years since its creation, but the most famous and best selling is undoubtedly 'The Teddy Bears Picnic' which is still so well known today that there is hardly an adult or a child anywhere who cannot sing at least a few lines of the lyrics. Strangely, the tune was originally written in 1907 without any words by an American composer named John W. Bratton as an amusing little jingle inspired by the Teddy Bear craze then in full flood. The tune became modestly popular with light orchestras, as background music for performing animals, and on occasions during Theodore Roosevelt's election campaign! It was not until 1930 that a British songwriter named Jimmy Kennedy was asked to put words to the tune and came up with the lyrics which, two years later, became an instant success when performed for the first time on BBC Radio. Since 1932 sheet music of the song has sold copies by the million, and one record of the tune alone (by Henry Hall and the BBC Dance Orchestra) has sold over three million copies. The sum total of record sales of the many versions of 'The Teddy Bears Picnic' made around the world is today believed to be in excess of twenty million copies!

(FACING PAGE) *The original sheet music of 'The Teddy Bears Picnic' by John W. Bratton (1907) and a photograph of the display made with bushes and flowers based on the famous song in the Parade Gardens, Bath. The sticker 'Paddington for P.M.' is just one of over 200 items bearing his name that have helped make Paddington the wealthiest of all Teddy Bears!*

PADDINGTON FOR P.M.

THE **TEDDY BEARS PICNIC**

BY

JOHN W. BRATTON

M. WITMARK & SONS.
186-188 SHAFTESBURY AVENUE. LONDON. W.C.
58. RUE DU FAUBOURG MONTMARTRE, PARIS.
NEW YORK.   SAN FRANCISCO.   CHICAGO.

Price 2/ net

THE RECORD MAKER

The record for creating the largest number of hand-made Teddy Bears is held by Mrs. Helen Henderson a delightful lady from Montreal in Canada who, at the time of writing, had made over 1,985 and was hard at work towards a grand total of 2,000! Mrs. Henderson donates the proceeds from the sale of her bears to charities (including the World Wildlife Fund) and says she derives enormous pleasure from creating them, giving each one its own individual characteristics. 'My bears', she says, 'like Moslem women, have to go veiled in public (in bags) as to see them is to desire them! My customers include chiropodists, nurses, hairdressers, postal workers, plumbers, golfers and grandmothers'. Asked what has made her keep adding to her record total (which should surely qualify her for a place in *The Guinness Book of Records?*), Mrs. Henderson said in 1975: 'It cannot be because my bears were always popular, because for the first five years they covered the guest room, unwanted. Only for the last two years have they become booked for six months ahead. So it must be because they are fun to make.' In a leaflet about herself and her work, Mrs. Henderson passes on nine hints and some general advice about making Teddy Bears which we think deserve an even wider audience:

1. Don't be easily satisfied with your bear.
2. Don't hestitate to re-do a loose joint (difficult!).
3. Or re-set a crooked ear (easy!).
4. Be sure that eager fingers can't pull out the eyes.
5. And as for noses, study the dogs you know.
6. Keep an open mind on materials and method.
7. Try to achieve the perfect bear.
8. Don't circulate your 'drop-outs'. They will lower your reputation. Cut your losses and try again.
9. If you find you are keen, list, number and photograph your Teddies.

She concludes: 'I advise the use of a thimble always, which advice is sometimes 100% not followed. And don't leave your thimble or even your needle inside. You may be sued. And even if you can't get enough used clean nylons for stuffing, don't take your husband's 'longs'. He may catch cold. And speaking of longs, husbands can be of tremendous help in turning those tough joints. And don't ever lose your needle even outside your bear. It may turn up inside someone you love!'

THE TEDDY BEAR CLUB

TEDDY Bear lovers and collectors now have their own international organisation called 'Good Bears of the World' which links *arctophiles* of every country in a giant 'hug' of friendship and dedication. The movement even has a special day each year, October 27, the anniversary of President Roosevelt's birthday, which is known as 'Good Bear Day'. Celebrations, in particular Teddy Bears' Picnics, mark this occasion, and funds are also raised to enable GBW to continue its work of donating Teddy Bears to hospitals for patients of all ages, to the elderly, and to all those who are felt to be in need of them. How this network of *arctophilists* has grown up is an interesting story. . . .

The tale goes back to the year 1951 when an American, Russell A. McLean, began to present Teddy Bears to his local hospital in Lima, Ohio. He was convinced of the little toy's ability to cheer up and comfort sick children and infants, and hoped that in

(BELOW) *Russell A. McLean, 'The Teddy Bear Man' who began the scheme for giving Teddy Bears to children in hospital, is seen here with one delighted young recipient!*

3,000 Circulation This Issue

BEAR TRACKS

OFFICIAL NEWSLETTER OF
THE GOOD BEARS OF THE WORLD

"Ladies and gentlemen and Teddy bears of the jury . . ."

DRAWING BY HANDELSMAN. 1979 THE NEW YORKER MAGAZINE, INC.

SPRING
1979

ALL WE NEED IS...

Our thanks to Jim Roeb of the Hippocrates Health Institute for this work of GBW computer art.

The Good Bears of the World
P.O. Box 8236
Honolulu, Hawaii 96815
USA
Return Postage Guaranteed

Have you offered a 'Bear Hug' today?

---

giving the bears he was providing—as he put it—'a little bit of Christmas spirit for youngsters every day of the year'. Such, indeed, was the success of his idea, that it was soon spreading beyond the confines of Ohio, and McLean himself became affectionately known across America as 'The Teddy Bear Man'.

At this same time, a mounting interest in Teddy Bears was also being manifested across the Atlantic in Britain. In 1962, Colonel Bob Henderson, a long time devotee and student of the Teddy Bear, was nominated 'President of the Teddy Bear Club' for his work in emphasising the role of the Teddy Bear in Western Society. Two authors were also gathering material for books: Margaret Hutchings, writer and toy maker, and Peter Bull, actor, traveller and author.

Margaret Hutching's *The Book of the Teddy Bear* appeared in 1964 and apart from briefly recording the early history of the Teddy Bear, gave detailed instructions on how to make a whole variety of different and attractive Teddy Bears. Peter Bull's book, however, was of a much more personal nature, and as his work in films and on the stage took him backwards and forwards across the Atlantic (he had important roles in 'Dr. Strangelove', 'Tom Jones' and the delightful 'Dr. Doolittle' as well as in notable plays like 'Waiting for Godot' and 'Luther') he gathered together a wealth of stories about Teddy Bears. Following one appearance on the American TV show 'Today' he received over 2,000 letters from Teddy Bear owners. When his book, *Bear With Me* (retitled *The Teddy Bear Book* in

Bear Tracks the interesting and informative publication of the 'Good Bears of the World' organisation.

America) appeared in 1969, he used it to explain the role of the Teddy Bear and went to considerable lengths to show that no one should be shy of confessing to own one or loving one. Arctophiles, he said, were far more numerous than was supposed, and came from all walks of life, famous as well as ordinary folk. (Mr. Bull has subsequently extensively revised this work and republished it in 1977 as *Peter Bull's Book of Teddy Bears*.)

Prompted by the work of these people on both sides of the Atlantic, Teddy Bears suddenly began to be featured in a whole variety of functions—at dances and on quiz programmes, at fairs and charity fetes, and even as mascots at sports meetings and football matches. They also began to increasingly appear in newspapers, magazines and in advertisements.

Colonel Henderson, who had been carefully studying this development of interest in the Teddy Bear, saw it as a phenomenon which he refers to as 'Teddy Bear Consciousness'.

(FACING PAGE) *James T. Ownby, 'Bearo No. 1', the Founder and Chairman of 'Good Bears of the World'. The initial 'T' in Jim's name stands for Theodore and he is said to be a distant relative of President Theodore Roosevelt, the man who started the whole Teddy Bear saga!*

'It is so deep-seated in the unconscious depth of the mind that it is practically inherent in the human psyche', he says. 'It has given rise to the expression "The Teddy Bear Club" which thus exists in the subconscious mind and is something much more subtle than a cult. As has been seen it does from time to time come into conscious existence and practical activity at various places all over the world. All those who have an affection for Teddy Bears and those who love them (arctophiles), who appreciate the value of the Teddy as an instrument in psychotherapy, and in this way are Teddy-Bear-Conscious, are automatically members, though at first they may not realise it.'

As a result, says Colonel Henderson, 'The Teddy Bear Club' has no subscription, no committee, no meeting place and no funds. It exists only universally in the subconscious mind, but an appreciation of the fact can be the first step towards bringing together those of a like mind into actual gatherings.

The year 1970 proved to be a most important one for the Teddy Bear, for it was then that what had hitherto been informal became formal with the founding of the 'Good Bears of the World'.

The driving force behind this new movement was an

Berne—'The Bear Town of Switzerland'. The old engraving above shows 'The Bears on the March' while the photograph below shows people dressed as bears during a recent festival. The Bear Pits on the opposite page are a great favourite with visitors of all ages, and the insert shows the town's coat of arms.

St Lukes Great Teddy Bear Gathering

Littlejohn Bear

Teddy Bears never die, they just grow old

1. To forever strive toward the preservation of the dignity of the brotherhood of Teddy Bears.
2. To love, honour and obey the master or mistress regardless of their age, sex or colour, whosoever fortune may result in my custody.
3. To provide through our presence even under threat of suffocation the feeling of safety and security to the young when things go bump in the night.
4. To forever preserve the patience toward exuberant treatment I may be exposed to in my lifetime.
5. To listen with patience to the words of the young and never grow tired of their attempts at conversation.
6. To forever represent a loving link with youth in the eyes and hearts of the not so young.
7. To meet at least once a year with fellow bears in friendly greeting in the cause of cementing the bonds of fellowship among Teddy Bears and their custodians.
8. To continue always in our efforts to maintain the universal appeal and worldwide popularity of the entire Teddy Bear race.

Mark Steele

(ABOVE) *A poster and copy of the 'Brotherhood of Teddy Bears Code' issued to mark the First Teddy Bear Convention in Auckland, New Zealand in August, 1979.* (BELOW) *One of the posters issued each year by GBW to mark 'Good Bear Day'.* (FACING PAGE) *Three of a whole range of very popular Teddy Bear post cards published in Germany.*

Good Bear Day

1977

American broadcaster and journalist, James T. Ownby, from Honolulu, who had been prompted to his action by Peter Bull's book *Bear With Me.* Selecting the anniversary of President Roosevelt's birthday, October 27, as a most appropriate day, and aided by Colonel Henderson, he founded GBW—as it subsequently became known— at a particularly suitable locality, Berne in Switzerland, 'Bear Town'. This was to be the headquarters of what he saw as an international humanitarian association pledged to form local groups (called dens) and raise money to buy Teddy Bears for sick children and those of any age in need of them. Each October 27 thereafter was to be marked as 'Good Bear Day'.

Such was the response to the new organisation that on 'Good Bear Day' 1973, it was officially inaugurated by a special gathering at the Bellevue Palace Hotel in Berne, after which the founders made a visit to the famous local *Bärengraben* (Bear Pits). In the subsequent newspaper reports of this event, one journalist wrote, 'The appeal of the Teddy Bear is universal. It is an international symbol of friendship and goodwill, and a bringer of comfort and affection in times of stress. Doctors say that Teddies do have considerable therapeutic value not only for children, but also for sick, lonely and elderly adults as well.' (As a matter of record, although Berne did continue as headquarters of GBW for some years thereafter, the centre has now been switched to Mr. Ownby's home town of Honolulu in Hawaii.)

In the years which followed, GBW has grown on both sides of the Atlantic recruiting new members all the time. Male members of the movement are known as 'Bearos', women as 'Bearines' and children as 'Cubs'. Today America has 1,500 members, the United Kingdom over 400, and there are also members in Canada, Australia, New Zealand, Germany, Austria, Norway,

France, Switzerland, and numerous other places such as Hong Kong and Korea.

To the members of GBW who worked to establish the movement in the early days, their greatest triumph to date was undoubtedly 'The Great Teddy Bear Rally' held on May 27, 1979 at Longleat in England which was reported in the press throughout the world (See cutting from TIME magazine). Over 15,000 people accompanied by more than 2,000 Teddy Bears turned up— many from abroad and places as far away as America, Europe, Australia and New Zealand—and during the day over 500 bears were donated to Dr. Barnardo's Homes. Hard on the heels of this event, "The First Teddy Bear Convention" was held in Auckland, New Zealand on August 23, and from August 27 to September 9, a group of Australians ran a similar rally in Bankstown Square, Sidney which attracted huge crowds. In Australia, too, at Toowoomba, Queensland, a Teddy Bear Museum has recently been opened. It houses over 200 bears ranging in size from a few inches to 9 ft 9 inches. Pride of the collection is a 73-year-old Teddy made in London in 1906 which is now regarded as 'The Oldest Teddy Bear in Australia'.

Even as this book has progressed from manuscript to finished volume, the story has continued with more and bigger rallies, gatherings and fund raising meetings. As Colonel Henderson has rightly commented, 'These events are giving the Teddy Bear the recognition it deserves. GBW is now fully "on the map" and Teddy is "On top of the World!".'

At 400-year-old Longleat House, a sea of Teddy bears obscures owners' faces; right, the Marquess of Bath with coroneted Teddy peer

Arctophilia Runs Amuck

A hug of Teddy bears gathers for a convention in Britain

Henry Frederick Thynne, sixth Marquess of Bath, tenth Viscount Weymouth, 13th Baron Thynne, 74 golden years of age, drew his Teddy bear Clarence to his breast and gave it a nice, warm hug. "They are," he sighed, "charming things to cuddle." Lord Bath ("Lordy" to his staff) was playing host last week at his 10,000-acre, 400-year-old stately Wiltshire home, Longleat House, where 8,000 grownups and tots were attending the world's largest gathering of Teddy bear lovers. It was a clear case of personal promotion by enterprising Businessman Lord Bath, who admitted all bears to the grounds free, but charged $1 per carload for humans. TIME *London Correspondent Art White, clutching only his notebook, observed the affair and sent this report:*

There were marmalade sandwiches and honey cakes, rapturous renditions of the ursine theme song *The Teddy Bears' Picnic,** animated bears powered by microelectronics, a first-aid tent for bear repair that admitted 54 patients, an actor reading Pooh stories, a competition for bears dressed to resemble the Marquess of Bath (robes and coronet, or red tie and cavalry twill trousers) and, above all, a joyful bonhomie not seen since Christopher Robin rescued Pooh from the Heffalump trap.

"Meet the fellas!" cried Virginia Walker, 54, of Anna Maria Island, Fla., who flew over for the rally with three of her Teddy bears, leaving the other 155 at home with her husband, a retired doctor who built a special room to accommodate them. "They call me the Landlady of Teddy Towers." A collector since childhood, Mrs. Walker explained: "Teddy bears make you feel good all over—they're the

*Sample lyric: "Ev'ry Teddy Bear who's been good/ Is sure of a treat today./ There's lots of marvelous things to eat,/ And wonderful games to play."

truest friend you can have." Mrs. Walker once left a treasured Teddy on a train in Switzerland. "They had to stop it. They were furious! And poor Chauncey got wrapped up in the bed sheets and went down a hotel laundry chute in Sicily. Since I didn't know how to say 'Teddy bear' in Italian, it took hours to find him."

Perhaps the oldest Teddy at the rally was the distinguished Sir Edward Bear, Bt. (so christened years ago by a curator of London's Victoria and Albert Museum), bought in 1904 in Switzerland by Eileen Rimer's grandfather. "He's one of the family," said Mrs. Rimer, who traveled from Essex with her husband and daughter Elizabeth, 21, owner of Sir Edward plus 25 other Teddies. Sir Edward, added Mrs. Rimer, is "tattered through much hugging and kissing, and lost his growl 40 years ago when my brothers bounced him off the ceiling, but we love him. I had a rather unhappy childhood, and he was my confidant. Teddies never answer back."

Elsie Chant, 60, brought her beat-up, geratic Teddy, only 2 in. tall, appropriately named Thread Bear. From Somerset came Computer Salesman Andrew Morrison, with his four small children, each breathlessly lugging an enormous Teddy, one wearing Dad's best tie. Said Morrison: "Teddies are an important emotional part of a kid's growing up, a security item. Sometimes mommies and daddies are too busy to listen. Teddy bears are never too busy."

Retired U.S. Air Force Colonel Tom Carhart, 61, a newcomer to Teddy collecting, acquired his first furry friend, Digger (who now wears Carhart's fighter pilot wings), a year ago in Australia, now has 28. Said Carhart, who flew from Amherst, Mass., for the rally: "My wife is as keen as I am. But my kids said, 'Oh, come on, Dad, you're not serious.' Now they're convinced I'm not balmy. They keep

their eyes open for Teddies for me."

Kid stuff? Nonsense, insisted British Actor-Author Peter Bull, 67, who has written two books about Teddy bears, and shares acclaim with Lieut. Colonel Robert Henderson, 75—head of the British branch of the Good Bears of the World, an association providing Teddy bears to hospitalized children—as the United Kingdom's leading arctophile. "Adults have a definite and equal need for the dear creatures," argued Bull. "There is a vast underground Teddy bear movement. We arctophiles are a touchy lot, and insults or ridicule by ignorant persons puts our hackles up. One is Teddy bear conscious in the same way other people are car, garden, tits, clothes, food or cat conscious." Agreed Henderson: "There's a widespread psychological need for Teddy bears." Even for cross-eyed Teddies, like the celebrated one named Gladly (from the hymn: "Gladly the Cross I'd bear").

Bull pointed out that Teddy bears (named after President Theodore Roosevelt, who, on an expedition to Mississippi in 1902, refused to shoot a bear cub) flew as wartime mascots in Spitfire cockpits, went into battle perched on guns, tanks and ships. One Teddy climbed the Matterhorn in its owner's knapsack. The late Donald Campbell set new speed records with his Mr. Woppit along for the ride. Britain's Poet Laureate, Sir John Betjeman, paid tribute to his Teddy, Archibald Ormsby-Gore, in his work *Summoned by Bells* ("Safe were those evenings of the pre-war world/ When [I] turned to Archibald, my safe old bear").

But not all Teddies are good bears. Bull recalled a remarkable case in which mysterious, heavy-breathing sounds were heard in a South London flat. The terrified occupants, two young women, feared that their Teddy bear was possessed by an evil spirit. A clergyman was called in to exorcise the demon, and duly pronounced the bear cured. Nonetheless, this was one naughty bear that was definitely not invited to Longleat's great Teddy bear rally. ■

"He doesn't know I took a lovely picture of him with his Teddy Bear at Longleat."

Century Club

Splittelse i BBF!

Informations redaktion har længe været stærkt splittet: skulle vi løfte sløret for den splittelse, der truer med at ødelægge alt, hvad bamserne har bygget op i Qvistgaard?

Vi ved, at vi vil blive beskyldt for at gå højrefløjens ærinde og blive sammenlignet med Berlingske Tidende — men de høje etiske idealer, der altid har præget Information, tvinger os til ikke at skjule sandheden.

Læs i reportager og interviews alt om *Splittelsen i Bamsernes Befrielsesfront!*

Desuden bringer vi en lang række læserindlæg om bamsesagen.

Sommersider 12 og 13.

(FACING PAGE) *A Giles cartoon inspired by the Longleat Rally, from the* Daily Express, *May 29, 1979. The South of England Building Society uses Teddy Bears as their motif to try and encourage children to save money with them through their 'Century Club'.*
A new organisation which has developed in Denmark is the Bamsernes Befrielsesfront *(BBF) or 'Teddy Bear Liberation Front' aimed at promoting love and kindness among adults. These illustrations are from the Copenhagen Newspaper,* Information, *which ran a special feature on the movement in its issue of July 20, 1979.*

GOOD BEARS OF THE WORLD

ANY reader interested in joining this very worthwhile organisation should write to one or other of the following addresses.

In the United Kingdom write to GBW (UK), 17, Barnton Gardens, Edinburgh, EH4 6AF, enclosing a stamped, addressed envelope at least 9 ins × 4 ins (23 cms × 10 cms) and 10p for brochure reply. Membership charges are £2.50 for Ordinary Membership; £3.50 for Ordinary Overseas Membership; and £5.00 for 'Benefactor' Membership. (In each case these are the minimum fees, but prospective members may care to donate more for GBW's voluntary work.)

American readers should write to The Good Bears of the World, P.O. Box 8236, Honolulu, Hawaii, 96815, United States of America, enclosing a stamped-addressed envelope and $8 in annual dues.

(ABOVE) *'The Teddy Bear Project' being run by the New Jersey State Federation of Women's Clubs to help Autistic Children by providing them with Teddy Bears.* (BELOW) *Leaflet prepared by the Bristol Dolls Hospital, one of numerous places helping to put sick teddies back on their paws again!*
(FACING PAGE) *A charming English postcard 'Teddy's Birthday Party' by Margaret Tempest; and below it a similar American card, 'Teddy's Picnic' by Lucy Rigg.*

Bristol Dolls Hospital

Tel: 0272-664368

If your Teddys broken
Do not make a fuss,
Just jump into a motor car
And bring it round to us

Do not be unhappy,
He'll only be there a while
He'll come out looking good as new,
And on his face, a great big SMILE

THE FANTASTIC APPEAL OF THE TEDDY BEAR

TO conclude this book, Colonel Bob Henderson explains his theory as to just how and why the Teddy Bear has come to have such a special place in human affections. He writes:

In her book *A History of Toys*, Lady Antonia Fraser asks 'What is it about the Teddy Bear which gives it this fantastic appeal? This is without doubt one of the most interesting psychological questions about the history of toys'. Also, in *The Book of the Teddy Bear*, Margaret Hutchings said 'the almost unfathomable appeal of the teddy bear is universal and to all ages'. While Peter Bull, in his book *Bear With Me*, said 'Teddy Bears seem destined to survive everything and emerge as a triumphant symbol'.

Consequently, Mrs. Eithne Kaiser, in her draft manuscript for a book on this subject, wrote 'This phenomenon is, in fact, so intense, so widespread, and so utterly taken for granted by adults, many of whom adhere to it themselves, that it demands some investigation both psychologically and mythologically for the bear, in the form of the teddy-bear has, oddly it seems, become our society's comforter. That almost all-pervading cuddly creature, which for many children is more important than any doll, and which remains with so many adults as something at once intrinsic and marginal to their most intimate life, acts *in loco parentis* as an archetypal mother/father understander-of-all, as indeed an original comforter, or Paraclete.'

Funnily enough, a clue to the solution of this mystery was quite lightheartedly though very rightly given by Peter Bull over the radio on March 2, 1977, when he was having a talk with Pete Murray in the 'Open House' programme and got onto the subject of teddy-bears. They both agreed that teddy-bears talk to you. 'It is in the way they look at you' they said.

Now when you come to consider this, you realise that this experience is, in fact, a feeling within you that is aroused by your sight of the teddy bear, though it speaks to you only in the sense of the significance it has for you, and this is largely connected with its form, which is that of a bear cub, soft and cuddly, so it appeals to your hunting and maternal, or paternal, instincts.

The Teddy does not, of course, actually speak to you. It only seems to do so, because in your mind you imagine it does. By means of its subtle appeal the teddy-bear excites your imagination, so that its significance as a symbol is impressed upon your inner consciousness. This region of your mind is where the archetypal Ideas in the realm of depth psychology assume symbolic form, which in our dreams often tend to take animal form, as they do in fairy tale and myth. Consequently, your vision of the teddy-bear is linked in the depth of your mind almost automatically with the archetypal symbolic bear that has figured so largely in ancient mythology and is still active in this area of the mind. So you become inwardly involved in this psychological archetypal activity.

As a symbol of love, affection and friendship the

ON MY only daughter's second birthday, she was given a large doll and a big brown teddy-bear. Thirty years later they are still in her old room. Her two little girls often play with them and on their last visit the eldest one wanted to take the teddy-bear home. "No," said my daughter. "She can't do that — it's mine!"
—Mrs. Smith, London.

Colonel Bob Henderson and 'Teddy Girl'—and on the facing page a photograph of Colonel Henderson and his brother and the bear they shared when they were all young!
The ageless appeal of Teddy—a cutting from the Sunday People, *December 23, 1979.*

"You'll be all right but I'm afraid teddy's had it"

" The sooner you get over having to sleep with a Teddy bear the better!"

teddy-bear appeals to the higher levels of your inner consciousness. This activates the better aspects of the universal archetypal symbolic bear (The Great Bear) and through this universal archetypal activity the teddy bear makes an appeal to the core of your inner being. This causes your inner voice to speak to your outer consciousness through the universal unconscious.

Consequently, when you are inwardly, or outwardly, talking to the teddy bear you are talking to your inner Self. The bear is merely the channel of this communication.

But, because your soul is linked with the Absolute, through this experience the 'personality' of the teddy-bear can affect you in such a way that it puts you in touch with the Infinite. Indeed, one professional clinical psychologist, Floyd R. Clark, has maintained that in this way the gap between your conscious mind and the universal unconscious, or 'racial unconscious' is bridged, so that you are enabled spiritually to become aware of a universal unity in all things when you are properly attuned to it.

When this happens you are not worshipping the bear, but using it as a psychological instrument, or medium, that is capable of establishing such communication. In a sort of a way it serves as a type of communion cup. One which will serve children well until they are old enough to partake in Christian Communion.

This is a perfectly natural thing to do, and is not in any way an abnormality. Those who consider *arctophiles* to be odd just do not realize this. The only peculiarity is the very personal reactions and associations in the experience, which are of course peculiar to each individual in the sense of belonging exclusively to them, not in the sense of being odd or strange.

So you see, the 'vast underground Teddy Bear movement' that Peter Bull says 'exists in the adult world' (see *Bear With Me*, page 88) is really a psychological movement in the mind rather than

Why not a Teddy Bear T-shirt with "HAPPINESS IS LOVING A TEDDY BEAR" or "TEDDY BEAR POWER" or "TEDDY BEARS ARE THE GREATEST" or. . . ?

Sunnie Henry
Selah, Washington

(ABOVE) *The Teddy Bear in cartoons—two amusing examples, from* She *magazine, July 1979, and* Sunday People, *December 30, 1979.* (LEFT) *A novel idea proposed by a reader of* Bear Tracks, *Fall 1979.*

Two photographs taken fifty years apart – but the love of children for their Teddy Bears is still the same. (ABOVE) *a postcard dating from 1927 and* (BELOW) *one of the unmistakable Alresford Bears.*

anything else. The factors underlying it lie far down in the realm of depth psychology; though largely concealed they are partly revealed in Jungian psychology.

I would explain it this way:

1 The subtle appeal of the teddy-bear exercises your imagination, and this links your conscious mind, through the archetypal symbols in the collective unconscious, with the spiritual realm of divine Ideas.

2 The activity of these archetypal Ideas, that is the serialization of creation, is inherent in all things, consequently images of them are engraved in the human soul, and reflected in the universal unconscious and express themselves through psychological archetypal activity.

3 The archetypal Idea of the bear, thus deep-seated in the soul, is constantly represented by the archetypal symbolic bear in the collective unconscious.

4 As the teddy-bear so well represents this archetypal symbolic bear, it is brought forward into the conscious mind, and so links the conscious mind with the divine archetypal Idea of the bear. The opening of this channel permits spiritual inspiration to flow through it.

5 The teddy-bear is grasped in psychic compensation and clung to for security. In this way it provides satisfaction for a widespread psychological need. This takes it right out of the classification of a soft toy.

6 When the teddy-bear is permitted to function in this way its significance can activate this psychological archetypal activity, and so have a powerful psychotherapeutic effect. This ultimately accounts for the fantastic appeal of the teddy-bear, which derives from the absolute function of the archetypal bear, its function as a surrogate for the mother as comforter, and for the Holy Ghost as The Comforter. (This comes about through association with the Great Bear constellation—*Ursa Major*—which was believed to be a representation of the 'Great Mother'. In medieval Christian symbolism, for example, the archetypal symbolic bear was considered to be in close association with the Creator, and to function as a symbol of both regeneration and resurrection.)

Thus, through its psychological links with both the

(ABOVE) *Teddy Bears were given to the children of the tragic Vietnamese boat people when a group of them were brought to Britain in June, 1979. Even though these youngsters had never seen a Teddy before, they proved an instant success as the photograph shows.*
(FACING PAGE) *Amusing story about the travel problems of big 'Benny the bear' and the outcome as reported in the* Daily Express *of September 10, 1979.*

BENNY'S TICKET TO RIDE

EXPRESS STAFF REPORTER

BENNY the bear's travelling problems are over. For yesterday the giant cuddly playmate of 12-year-old Lesley Ashley was issued with a free bus pass.

The bulky bear—4ft 6in on his woolly paws—caused a rumpus when Lesley took him by bus to her school sports day. *The conductor made her buy him a ticket.*

Lesley, who had only 10p for her own round-trip fare, paid 5p for herself and 3p for the teddy — and that meant a weary walk back to her home in Toner Avenue, Hebburn, Tyne and Wear, with Benny in her arms.

But when the Northern Bus Company heard about the sad saga they agreed to make amends.

At a ceremony yesterday Benny was presented with Bus Pass No. 0001 which allows him to travel free on any of the company's 850 vehicles.

Bulky Bear gets free bus pass

Mr Peter Shipp, assistant traffic manager, said : " We don't like this sort of thing happening to bears and we do not want it to happen again."

And a delighted Lesley said : " It's nice to know the next time we go for a ride my teddy will travel free."

The bear-er

0001 Benny's special bus pass reads : " This pass entitles the bear-er to free travel on all Northern services when accompanied by a human fare-paying passenger. Not transferable to other bears."

And it's signed, of course. With a paw print. . . .

Lesley shows Benny's pass complete with paw print

"I don't care if she did have to pay the fare for her Teddy, I'm not giving it my seat"

instincts (hunting, maternal and paternal) and the inner knowledge of the soul (gnosis), and by means of the influential significance of the archetypal symbolic bear, that it represents, the GBW gift teddy-bear can in many different ways serve as a powerful source of comfort, consolation and encouragement, and be highly effective as a gift of friendship, a token of love, a symbol of hidden strength, a transmitter of spiritual forces, as well as a pointer to unfolding perfection.

In so doing it can help to dispense 'a little bit of Christmas spirit' practically every day universally.

Finally, the important point to keep in mind is the fact that the Teddy Bear functions as a symbol. It is what it represents that counts. From the psychologist's point of view it is a representation of an 'archetypal' symbol in the form of a bear. From the mythologist's point of view it is a 'mythological' symbol in the form of an 'effect image' that is one which functions mystically.

C. G. Jung maintained that the imageries of mythology and religion serve positive life-furthering ends. They are energy releasing and directing signs, which inspire and move one in a particular way. That is why the GBW gift Teddy Bear can function in many ways and bring to its owner feelings of security, contentment and happiness.

In this way Teddy truly becomes a 'Good Bear of the World'.

PHONING IS BUSINESS—AMERICAN STYLE SO CALL, FOR BUSINESS' SAKE!

Americans really like to do business by phone, because it's informal, easy and instant. They like direct conversation that makes the big points, answers the tough questions and settles the deal. A telephone call to America is an investment that pays off in big dividends.

Dial direct whenever you can, for instant connections, and check the schedule at left so you call at the right time for American offices or homes, whatever time zone they're in. Phoning makes you more than just a name, it makes you a friend. And friends can do better business.

BUSINESS HOURS*				
Continental European Time	American Working Hours			
	Eastern	Central	Mountain	Pacific
3 P.M.	9 A.M.			
4 P.M.	10 A.M.	9 A.M.		
5 P.M.	11 A.M.	10 A.M.	9 A.M.	
6 P.M.	12 P.M.	11 A.M.	10 A.M.	9 A.M.
7 P.M.	1 P.M.	12 P.M.	11 A.M.	10 A.M.
8 P.M.	2 P.M.	1 P.M.	12 P.M.	11 A.M.
9 P.M.	3 P.M.	2 P.M.	1 P.M.	12 P.M.
10 P.M.	4 P.M.	3 P.M.	2 P.M.	1 P.M.
11 P.M.	5 P.M.	4 P.M.	3 P.M.	2 P.M.

 Bell System

TODAY'S THE DAY THAT TEDDY BEAR CAUSES PANIC.

(ABOVE) *Recent advertisement used by Bell Telephones in America, and the new-look symbol for the drinking straws manufactured by Premier Industries Inc. A Teddy Bear has been their symbol for almost 50 years.* (LEFT) *Oh, the shame of it! A survey shows Teddy as one of the worst culprits of drain blockage.*
(FACING PAGE) *Teddy Bears in Space! Cover artwork for* Earthman's Burden *a novel by Poul Anderson and Gordon R. Dickson about the Hokas 'a race of Teddy Bear-like aliens with the astounding ability to transform outdated Earth stories into riotous real life adventures!'*

TEDDY BEAR TALES

BOARDING the Channel ferry at Calais clutching my adored Teddy called Fifi, the Captain called: "Hello Goldilocks, what have you done with the other two?" — *Mrs. M. Pike, Peterborough.*

✳

WHEN your lover has left and you are lonely in bed, there's a lot to be said for the company of Ted.—*Marion Laine, West London.*

✳

FOLLOWING my first proper haircut my mother said: "It will grow again." I cut Teddy's hair. When I found his wouldn't I wept for ages.—*John Fox, Dudley, West Midlands.*

✳

ME and my Teddy were going on a honeymoon but teacher said you can't marry a Teddy. I prefer my Teddy to girls. — *Neil Farrell, Class 6, St. Margaret's Primary School, Dunfermline.*

✳

MY THEN six-year-old daughter and Teddy walked through security at Heathrow, set off the alarm and were grabbed. Teddy's "growler" upset the system.—*Mrs. Doreen Jones, Hanham, Bristol.*

MY friend's little girl has given the name Gladly to her beloved teddy bear, which happens to be cross-eyed. Asked to explain the name, she said: "We sing about my teddy in church. It's a hymn called 'Gladly my cross-eyed bear'."

And what a good hymn it is—"Gladly my cross i'd bear"!—*John Mullis, Shaftesbury, Dorset.*

✳

WAR veteran flying teddy, 53 years old, ninety sorties as aircrew mascot to credit (and never shot down) seeks invitation to picnic or Press recognition.—*Betty Luke, Brough, N. Humberside.*

✳

FATHER TED lost an arm in a Zeppelin raid in 1917; was my constant companion through World War Two and knows more secrets than MI5. — *Mrs. Patricia Holmes, Sanderstead, S. Croydon.*

WHAT a shock seeing my young daughter putting her Teddy Bear into the concrete mixer full of cement. She thought it was a washing machine. — *Mrs. V. Davidson, Jarrow, Tyne and Wear.*

✳

YEARS ago, Mum washed my Teddy and pegged him out. Later on, there were two ears on the line and one body in the mud! — *Mrs. L. F. Johnston, Portsmouth.*

MY Teddy bear is six feet tall, The Cuddliest Teddy of them all, He shares my troubles, makes me laugh, Hubbie bear, my better half! — *Mrs. Patricia Hill, Camberwell, South London.*

✳

TEDDY from my first love (who went away) survived emigration, divorce, hardship. I met his giver again after 30 years and I am 18 again. —*Ursula Sturgess, Huntingdon, Cambs.*

The winning letters in a competition run by the Sunday Mirror's '*Big Ted' to find the best readers' stories about their Teddy Bears. March 18, 1979.*

Teddy bears and under 5's travel free on British Rail

Yes, from this summer onwards you can take your under 5's out for nothing!
From Sunday 17th June, British Rail puts up the age limit for free travel by two full years. From 3 to 5.

This means you can take your under 5's with you free on any trip by train. A day out at the seaside. Or sight-seeing. Or visiting Gran. And your family holiday.
Under 5's eat free too. Travellers-Fare meals in the restaurant car are now free ___ under 5.
___ l details of money-saving tickets for Mum and Dad, get the booklet ___ e your rail ticket. Free from principal stations or British Rail travel

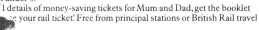

≥ British Rail

Have a good ti

Teddy is established as one of the most popular characters in British advertising—here are just three typical examples from British Rail, The Electricity Council and The National Children's Home. We expect to be collecting a lot more such ads in the future!

ACKNOWLEDGEMENTS

Our greatest debt of gratitude is to Colonel Bob Henderson who generously donated his time, knowledge and extensive library of material and illustrations thereby making our task easier and, we believe, helping to create a better book. Similarly Peter Bull in England and Jim Ownby in America were kindness itself. Among other individuals we should like to thank are Sir John Betjeman, Patrick Matthews, Mark Michtom of the Ideal Toy Corporation, Mr I. A. Schmeizl of Margarete Steiff Gmbh, Denis Gifford, Graham Webb, Herbert R. Collins, Lucy Rigg and Stewart Ferguson. The following organisations are also to be thanked for allowing their material to be used in the book: *Daily Mail*, *Sunday Express*, *Daily Express*, *Sunday Mirror*, *Sunday People*, *The Observer*, *Glasgow Evening Times*, *Eastern Daily Press*, *TV Times*, *Investor's Chronicle*, *Woman's Weekly*, *The Veterinary Record*, *Punch*, D. C. Thompson, Western Publishing Corporation, Fleetway Publications, *Art & Antiques Magazine*, *Which? Magazine*, *She Magazine*, *Life*, Avon Books, Wm. Collins' Sons & Co Ltd., Methuen Ltd., Macdonald & Janes, Gollancz, George G. Harrap, Macmillan, The Swiss Tourist Office, London Express News & Feature Service, Keystone Picture Agency, The Medici Society, British Rail, The National Children's Home, The Electricity Council, Dean's Childsplay Toys, Merrythought Ltd., The British Film Institute, Hanna-Barbera Films, Walt Disney Pictures, Warner Bros. Finally, the patient and helpful staffs of the London Library, The British Museum, The Smithsonian Institution, and Bruton Photography who photographed much of the material herein—and, of course, all those *arctophiles* starting with Jonna Koster of the Netherlands who turned our publisher on to the idea of this book, and all those many others who provided the photographs and information about their Teddies and, as much as anyone, made this book possible.